THE — 21-DAY REVIVAL COOKBOOK

80 MEALS TO LOSE WEIGHT, INCREASE ENERGY AND BEAT INFLAMMATION

DR. AMANDA LEVITT

UpWellness
Nutrient-Rich Living

HOW TO USE THIS COOKBOOK:

The recipes that you'll find within this book were prepared to complement and help guide you through your meals during each phase of the 21-Day Revival Program and beyond. As you know, the program is structured into three distinct phases, each one with its own prescriptive guidelines for foods to include and foods to avoid. Although each phase has its own rules and regulations, there is also some significant overlap in which foods are incorporated within each phase. In other words, some recipes might be suitable for phase two and phase three...so if this book was organized into recipes for each phase, you would either miss some recipes or have some recipes listed more than once. So...In order to make this cookbook as user-friendly as possible, we have decided to label each one according to which phase (or phases) that it is appropriate for. Additionally, most of the recipes in this book can be slightly modified to suit whichever phase of the program you are in.

Here's a quick reminder and summary about each phase:

PHASE ONE: Days 1-7

This first phase takes care of some important internal housekeeping. You can think of it as the "basic clean up." In Phase One you will be eating a clean diet that includes lots of familiar foods so you will not feel hungry or deprived. Your diet will be densely packed with nutrients and you'll be putting the focus on eliminating the common triggers of inflammation and increasing the overall nutrient density of your diet.

You will phase out "junk" foods and drinks, especially those that contain high fructose corn syrup. You will eliminate white carbohydrates and replace them with whole grain sources. You will learn why it is critical that you cut out factory-farmed animal products, but you'll be free to eat "clean" meat, poultry, fish, eggs, and dairy products. You will be avoiding processed foods with their long lists of chemical ingredients, and will be building meals based on a list of whole, single-ingredient foods.

PHASE TWO: Days 8-14

We are going to kick it up a notch this week! During this period, you will be hitting your stride and developing the dietary and lifestyle habits that are part of your long-term nutritional goals. You'll begin to add in more plant-based superfoods and decrease your animal protein significantly. You'll cut out refined grains entirely, learn how to incorporate whole grains, and an even greater percentage of your food will be coming from your own kitchen.

It does not need to be a vegetarian or vegan diet, but it is power-packed with plant-based foods which are associated with decreased inflammation and reduced risk of chronic disease. This is the way that the longest-lived people in the world tend to eat, so it is clearly a long-term, sustainable solution.

Phase Two is really important to get comfortable with because it is the portion of this program that most closely resembles the eating pattern that you should strive to continue when this program is over.

PHASE THREE: Days 15-21

Phase Three begins with a big weekend event: a 48-hour liquid only fast! For two days, you will be consuming an abundance of easily digestible nutrients in the form of blended drinks, smoothies, juices, soups, broths, and teas. Liquid nutrition for 48 hours is a safe and effective way to jumpstart your anti-inflammatory biochemistry, without compromising your nutrition. Your immune system uses vitamins, minerals, and phytonutrients for fuel, so optimizing the absorption of these compounds is an excellent way to enhance the anti-inflammatory process.

In the remainder of Phase Three, you'll be eating a plant-based diet, primarily vegetarian with a little twist (small amounts of premium animal protein will be allowed). You will be eliminating wheat, gluten, and most dairy products as well. If you think you might have a dairy intolerance, you can eliminate dairy completely during this phase. It will be a big change from the way you used to eat. During this period, you will get acquainted with some new foods and flavors, and begin to notice what it feels like to be optimally nourished.

Along with the improvements that you'll feel in your body, like increased energy, better sleep, improved mood, and better digestion, you'll also begin to assimilate the dietary and lifestyle improvement that you've been learning into a daily routine that will ultimately become a longer-term, sustainable plan for the future.

We tried to make it as easy as possible for you to have nutritious and delicious options for each day of the program. Our hope is that some of these recipes become your own family favorites long after you've completed the 21 Day Revival Program.

Bon Appétit!

A few notes before we begin:

1   **We're all human:** We're pretty sure that everyone who chooses to do this
    program is a *Homo sapien*...in other words, we're all human. But beyond that
    important similarity, we are all unique. We have different preferences for
    taste and texture. Some people experience negative reactions to foods that
    make other people feel great. Some of us are hungry in the morning, while
    others feel sick with a big meal to start the day. Some of us love to cook, while
    others don't know how to make toast. And some of us like simple foods,
    while others prefer an elaborate meal. It is okay to tailor this plan to suit your
    own individual preferences.

2   **Easy or Elaborate:** Some of the recipes in this book are quick and easy,
    others are more elaborate. If you like a simple roasted sweet potato, that's
    great. And if you're inclined to turn that sweet potato into an impressive
    sweet potato casserole...that's great too. Similarly, you might be a person who
    does just fine with a bowl of oatmeal with some fresh fruit and cinnamon...
    but if you want to branch out a bit, you'll enjoy the baked oatmeal recipe
    that you'll find in the grains section. We encourage exploration and
    experimentation with foods and flavors that might be new to you.

3   **Weight Loss:** Many people start this program with a goal of losing weight. Cutting out sweetened beverages, white flour, refined sugars, and other nutrient-poor foods is an important first step for successful weight loss. The goal of this program is to teach you how to eat well for long term health AND long term healthy weight management. If you have weight loss as one of your goals for this program, it's important that you remember this: You CAN eat too much good food. The meals and recipes presented here are based on nutrient dense, minimally processed foods. They can all be part of a long-term healthy eating pattern...but only if you keep your portion sizes reasonable. Keep the "food rules" on page 17 of your 21 Day Revival book in mind and remember to eat only during a 8-12 hour period each day and...no seconds.

4   **Where's the Beef?** The 21 Day Revival program is a guide to anti-inflammatory eating and an entry point for a transition to a more plant-based diet. Most people who choose to do this program do not need much help finding new or different ways to cook meat or poultry, but they do need help learning how to prepare and eat more plants. As such, this cookbook focuses primarily on plant-based dishes. It is not exclusively vegetarian or vegan, but the recipes are *mostly* plant-based. That doesn't mean you necessarily have to exclude animal proteins completely. As described in the 21 Day Revival, high-quality fish, beef, poultry, dairy, and eggs can absolutely be a healthy part of your diet and many of the recipes included in this cookbook have room for animal protein options.

GRAINS

PAGE	RECIPE	PHASE 1	2	3
19	Brown Rice	✓	✓	✓
20	Asian Rice Salad	✓	✓	✓
21	Vegetable Fried Rice	✓	✓	✓
23	Kasha (Roasted Buckwheat)	✓	✓	✓
24	Simple Kasha with Onions and Mushrooms	✓	✓	✓
25	Quinoa	✓	✓	✓
26	Quinoa Salad With Roasted Sweet Potato and Toasted Pepitas	✓	✓	✓
27	Sunny Quinoa Salad with Lemon and Garlic	✓	✓	✓
28	Honey Lime Quinoa Fruit Salad	✓	✓	✓
29	Farro	✓	✓	
30	Bulgur	✓	✓	
31	Mediterranean Tabouli	✓	✓	
33	Hearty Oatmeal With Fruit and Nuts	✓	✓	✓
35	Easy Baked Oatmeal	✓	✓	✓
36	Make Your Own Sushi	✓	✓	✓
37	Buddha Bowl (with three dressings)	✓	✓	✓
42	Nut Loaf	✓	✓	✓
44	Almond Butter Chia Pudding	✓	✓	✓
45	Vanilla Cinnamon Chia Pudding	✓	✓	✓

VEGETABLES

BEANS, LENTILS, AND CHICKPEAS

PAGE	RECIPE	PHASE 1	2	3
71	One-Pot Tuscan White Bean Stew	✓	✓	
73	Sweet Potato Black Bean Burritos	✓		
75	Three Sisters Stew	✓	✓	
77	Black Bean and Mango Salad	✓	✓	
79	Crispy Butter Beans and Broccoli	✓	✓	
81	West African Peanut Soup With Chickpeas	✓	✓	
83	Mexican Bean and Polenta Casserole	✓	✓	
85	Red Lentil Soup With Coconut Milk and Lime	✓	✓	✓
87	Red Bean and Quinoa Chili	✓	✓	
89	Butter Beans with Pesto, Artichoke Hearts and Sundried Tomatoes	✓	✓	
90	Roasted Sweet Potato and Chickpea Salad	✓	✓	✓
92	Chana Masala	✓	✓	
94	White Bean and Kale Minestrone	✓	✓	
96	Lemony Chickpeas	✓	✓	✓
97	Sweet and Spicy Barbeque Beans	✓	✓	
98	Quesadillas (Simple and Fancy)	✓		
99	Spicy Tortilla Soup	✓		
101	Panna Cotta	✓		
103	Roasted Chickpeas	✓	✓	✓

SOY: TOFU, MISO, TEMPEH

PAGE	RECIPE	PHASE 1	2	3
106	Sweet Potato Cauliflower, and Tofu Fajita	✓	✓	✓
107	Hearty Miso Soup	✓	✓	✓
109	Hawaiian Barbeque Tofu Bowl	✓	✓	✓
111	Tofu Scramble	✓	✓	✓
112	Tofu and Broccoli Stir-Fry	✓	✓	✓
114	Tempeh Tacos With Avocado Corn Salsa	✓		
116	Veggie Pot Pie With Tofu	✓		
118	Crispy Tofu With Peanut Sauce	✓	✓	✓
120	Sesame Crusted Tofu With Garlic Spinach	✓	✓	✓

EGGS AND DAIRY

PAGE	RECIPE	PHASE 1	2	3
123	Egg and Vegetable Strata	✓		
125	Sweet Potato Waffles	✓		
126	Grab and Go Veggie Egg Muffins	✓	✓	✓
128	Puff Pancake With Fruit	✓		
130	Huevos Rancheros	✓		
131	Yogurt Parfait	✓	✓	✓
132	Vegetable Frittata	✓	✓	✓

SPECIAL SECTION FOR LIQUID ONLY FAST DAYS:

PAGE	RECIPE	PHASE 1	2	3
135	Nut-Berry Protein Shake	✓	✓	✓
136	Miso Broth	✓	✓	✓
137	Carrot Ginger Soup	✓	✓	✓
138	Blender Green Juice	✓	✓	✓
139	Hibiscus Tea	✓	✓	✓
140	Lemon Ginger Detox Tea	✓	✓	✓
141	Carrot Apple Ice Blend	✓	✓	✓
142	Pomegranate Cherry Smoothie	✓	✓	✓
143	Tropical Smoothie Bowl	✓	✓	✓
144	Peanut Butter Smoothie	✓	✓	✓

WHOLE GRAINS

What is a "whole" grain?

A whole grain is the entire seed of a grain plant that include the bran (the outer husk), the germ (the kernel inside that will sprout into a new plant), and the endosperm (the starchy portion of the seed that nourishes the germ as it grows). When a whole grain is refined, the bran and germ are removed, leaving only the starchy endosperm.

Whole grains are healthier because they include all three parts of the grain.

- **Refined grains** are processed to remove beneficial nutrients and fiber. Examples include white flour or corn syrup which are then used to make products like bread, pastries, snack foods, and sugary beverages. Refined grains are excluded in the 21 Day Revival program because they promote inflammation. These foods have a high "glycemic index" which means that they are rapidly converted into sugar in the bloodstream, which triggers a sudden spike in insulin. Rapid rises in insulin cause the body to abruptly drop blood sugar levels below the resting level, which causes a powerful urge to eat to restore blood sugar levels. This vicious cycle of high blood sugar, then crashing due to insulin, contributes to inflammation, insulin resistance, and obesity.

- **Whole grains** are minimally-processed, high in fiber, and nutrient-rich foods. These healthy carbs contain fiber which slows the sugar transport into the bloodstream, which keeps insulin levels more stable. Not only do whole grains have a more balanced effect on blood sugar, they also contain more vitamins, minerals, fiber, and healthy phytochemicals than refined grains. Fiber-rich whole grains also increase the bulk of the meal, making you feel fuller, which can help moderate the amount of food you eat. More fiber promotes healthy weight management. Fiber also provides food to support beneficial bacteria in the gut, while supporting heart health through its cholesterol-lowering actions.

This cookbook contains recipes that use unrefined whole grains like brown rice, quinoa, millet, farro, barley, bulgur, oats, or buckwheat (kasha).

For weight loss, keep serving sizes of grains to about ½ cup of cooked grain per meal.

BROWN RICE

Brown rice is a fiber-rich grain that is a good source of protein, micronutrients (like folic acid), and minerals, such as selenium.

Time: 45 minutes
Yields: 2 ½ cups

PHASE   1   2   3

1 cup of brown rice (our favorite is short grain brown rice)

Pinch of sea salt

1 ¾ cup of water

1   Place rice in pot with salt and water.

2   Bring to a boil.

3   Cover pot and reduce to a simmer for 45-50 minutes or until all water is absorbed.

4   Do not stir rice while cooking.

5   Fluff with fork and serve.

ASIAN RICE SALAD

Toasted sesame oil and balsamic vinegar make this simple grain salad pop with flavor.

Prep time: 15 minutes if using pre-cooked rice
Makes: 4-6 servings

PHASE 1 2 3

3 cups of cooked brown rice

1 cup of fresh or frozen peas

1 cup of fresh
or frozen edamame

2 teaspoons of olive oil

1 onion, chopped

1 carrot, diced

1 stalk of celery, chopped

Toasted sesame seeds (optional)

DRESSING:

2 tablespoons of olive oil

¼ cup fresh-squeezed lemon juice

1 teaspoon of tamari
or soy sauce

1 teaspoon of toasted sesame oil

1 ½ teaspoons
balsamic vinegar

1 Cook brown rice.

2 Whisk together dressing ingredients. Then, pour over warm rice, toss together, and set aside.

3 Heat the oil in a skillet and sauté onion until soft.

4 Add peas, edamame, carrot, and celery to onions, and sauté for 3-5 minutes.

5 Add vegetable mixture to the dressed rice.

6 Toss together and sprinkle with toasted sesame seeds (optional).

VEGETABLE FRIED RICE

Fried rice is a versatile dish that can be made with any combination of leftover grains like rice or farro, and any of your favorite vegetables. The key is to cook each vegetable in the pan and transfer to a bowl in order to avoid overcooking any ingredient. No need to clean pan between each vegetable. Once all the vegetables are cooked, you add them back into the pan to combine with the rice. (Omit peppers for phase 3.)

Prep Time: 20 minutes, with cooked rice
Makes: 4 servings

PHASE 1 2 3

1-2 tablespoons of olive oil for stir frying

1 medium onion, chopped

1 red bell pepper, chopped

½ pound green beans or asparagus, cut into 1-inch pieces

1 cup fresh or thawed frozen peas

1 cup bean sprouts

1 tablespoon minced garlic

1 tablespoon peeled and minced fresh ginger

3-4 cups cooked brown rice (or other cooked grain)

2 eggs, lightly beaten (optional)

¼ cup cooking sherry, white wine or stock

2 tablespoons soy sauce or tamari

1 tablespoon dark sesame oil

¼ cup chopped fresh cilantroleaves for garnish (optional)

1. Add 1 tablespoon of olive oil in a large skillet over a high heat. Add onion and bell pepper and cook, stirring occasionally, until they soften and begin to brown (about 3 minutes).

2. Lower the heat if the mixture starts to brown too quickly. Transfer the vegetables to a bowl.

3. Add the green beans or asparagus and cook, again over high heat, stirring occasionally, until nicely browned and just tender (about 5 minutes). Add them to the bowl with the onions and peppers.

4. Add peas to the skillet and then add the bean sprouts and cook for about 1 minute and then add to the bowl of vegetables.

5. Put the remaining oil in the skillet, add garlic and ginger. Stir to avoid burning. Add the rice or other grain, a little at a time, using a spatula to break up the clumps, and toss it with the oil. When all the rice is added, make a well in its center and break the eggs (optional) into it. (If you are using eggs, first scramble them with a spatula to cook, then stir to incorporate them into the rice).

6. Return the bowl of vegetables to the pan and use the spatula to combine vegetables, rice, and egg mixture.

7. Add the wine, sherry or stock and cook, stirring, for about a minute.

8. Add the soy sauce and sesame oil, then taste and add salt and pepper if necessary.

9. Turn off the heat, stir in the cilantro, and serve.

KASHA (ROASTED BUCKWHEAT)

Kasha is a type of buckwheat with a unique nutty flavor. In addition to being gluten-free (despite the name buckwheat), it's a great source of fiber, flavonoids, and minerals like magnesium.

Prep time: 25 minutes
Yields: 2 ½ to 3 cups

PHASE 1 2 3

1 cup of Kasha

2 cups of water

Pinch of sea salt

1 Bring water and salt to a boil.

2 Add Kasha.

3 Cover pot and reduce heat to simmer for 15-20 minutes.

4 Fluff with a fork and serve.

SIMPLE KASHA WITH ONIONS AND MUSHROOMS

Prep Time: 15-20 minutes
Makes: 4-6 servings

PHASE 1 2 3

1-2 tablespoons of olive oil

1 yellow onion, chopped
or 1 bunch of scallions
cut into 1-inch sections

1 cup of sliced mushrooms
(button, crimini, shitake, etc)

1 cup of cooked kasha

Salt and pepper to taste

1   Add oil to skillet and saute
onions or scallions for about
5 minutes and then add
mushrooms, stirring until
golden brown and soft (about 10
minutes).

2   Add cooked kasha, mix well
with onions and mushrooms.

3   Salt and pepper to taste.

QUINOA

A gluten-free grain that's a great source of fiber, protein, and essential amino acids.

Prep Time: 20-25 minutes
Yields: 2 ½ to 3 cups

PHASE | 1 | 2 | 3

1 cup of Quinoa

Pinch of sea salt

1 ¾ cups of water

1   Rinse quinoa with warm water and drain to reduce the bitter taste.

2   Place rinsed quinoa, salt, and water in a pot.

3   Bring to a boil.

4   Cover and reduce heat to a low simmer for 15-20 minutes, until all water is absorbed.

5   Fluff with a fork before serving.

QUINOA SALAD WITH ROASTED SWEET POTATO AND TOASTED PEPITAS

Roasted sweet potatoes and toasted pumpkin seeds combine deliciously together to make this dish a favorite!

Prep Time: 45 minutes
Serves: 4-6

PHASE **1** **2** **3**

2 ½ cups of cooked quinoa

2 medium sweet potatoes, chopped into bite-sized pieces

Sea salt, pepper

1 small onion

¼ cup extra virgin olive oil

2 tablespoons of balsamic or red wine vinegar

½ teaspoon of garlic powder

¼ cup fresh parsley, chopped

¼ cup toasted pumpkin seeds (pepitas)

1 Preheat oven to 400°F.

2 Toss sweet potato with 1-2 tablespoons olive oil and sprinkle with salt.

3 Roast until golden brown and easily pierced with a fork (about 35 minutes). Then, set roasted sweet potato aside.

4 Sauté the onions until soft, about 5 minutes.

5 Add roasted sweet potatoes, parsley, and sautéed onions to quinoa.

6 Whisk olive oil and vinegar together, add salt and pepper and garlic powder to taste.

7 Pour over quinoa and toss together gently.

8 Garnish with toasted pumpkin seeds.

SUNNY QUINOA SALAD WITH LEMON AND GARLIC

This tangy grain salad is crunchy, colorful and delicious. Perfect for a picnic side dish or a healthy lunch on the go.

Prep Time: 30 minutes
(15 minutes if using cooked quinoa)
Serves: 4-6

PHASE 1 2 3

1 cup dry quinoa

1 3/4 cup water

1/2 teaspoon sea salt

1/2 cup carrots, chopped

1/3 cup parsley, minced

1/4 cup sunflower seeds

4 cloves garlic, minced

1/4 cup freshly squeezed lemon juice

1/4 cup extra-virgin olive oil

2 tablespoons tamari or soy sauce

1 Rinse quinoa with warm water and drain through a fine strainer.

2 Place quinoa, salt, and water in a 2-quart pot.

3 Bring water to boil, reduce heat to low, cover and let simmer 15-20 minutes, until all the water is absorbed.

4 Let quinoa stand for 5-10 minutes uncovered, then fluff with a fork.

5 Place cooked quinoa in a large bowl. Add carrots, seeds, and parsley to quinoa. Mix thoroughly.

6 Combine garlic, lemon juice, olive oil and tamari; pour over quinoa and toss well.

7 Serve at room temperature or chilled.

HONEY LIME QUINOA FRUIT SALAD

Quinoa is a complete protein, which means it provides all nine essential amino acids necessary for good health. It also happens to add a tasty crunch to this fruit salad. The fresh pieces of fruit are glazed with honey and lime which add a sweet and tangy flavor.

PHASE **1** **2** **3**

1 cup quinoa, cooked

1 cup blackberries

1 cup blueberries

1 1/2 cup strawberries, sliced or diced

1 mango, diced

1/4 cup raw honey

2 tablespoons lime juice

1 In a large bowl, combine all of the fruit with the quinoa.

2 Make the glaze by combining honey and lime juice in a small bowl.

3 Drizzle the glaze over the fruit salad, tossing well to coat.

FARRO

Farro is highly nutritious ancient grain that originated in Italy. It has a chewy texture and a nutty taste. Farro is rich in protein, fiber, B vitamins, and minerals, like zinc and magnesium.

Prep Time: 25-30 minutes
Yields: 3 cups

PHASE 1 2

1 cup Farro

Pinch of sea salt

3 cups of water or stock

1 Rinse and drain Farro.

2 Bring water and salt to a boil.

3 Reduce heat to a simmer and cook uncovered for 25-30 minutes.

4 Drain off any excess water.

5 Fluff with a fork and serve.

BULGUR

Bulgur is a whole grain made from cracked wheat. It is a traditional, staple grain in the mediterranean diet. Bulgur is low in fat, but high in plant-based protein, heart-healthy fiber, and minerals like iron, magnesium, and manganese.

(Note: Bulgur does naturally contain gluten)

Prep Time: 20 minutes
Yields: 3 cups

PHASE 1 2

1 cup of bulgur

Pinch of sea salt

1 cup of water

1 Bring water and salt to a boil.

2 Add bulgur.

3 Cover and remove from heat.

4 Let stand covered for 10-15 minutes.

5 Fluff with a fork before serving.

6 Add a few drops of olive oil to cooked grain to avoid clumping.

MEDITERRANEAN TABOULI

Tabouli is a classic Mediterranean salad featuring fresh parsley, mint, lemon, and whole-grain bulgur.

Prep Time: 30 minutes
Makes: 4 servings

PHASE 1 2

1 cup of bulgur

1 cup of boiling water

½ cup chopped
fresh parsley

2 scallions,
chopped including greens

½ cup cucumbers,
chopped in bite-sized pieces

½ cup tomato,
chopped into small pieces

¼ cup mint, chopped

DRESSING:

¼ cup freshly
squeezed lemon juice

3 tablespoons of
extra virgin olive oil

1 tablespoon of tamari
or soy sauce

1. Place uncooked bulgur in a mixing bowl.

2. Pour boiling water over the grain and cover.

3. Let covered grain stand for 15 minutes, then fluff with a fork.

4. Once the grain has cooled to room temperature, add chopped parsley, scallions, cucumber, tomato, and mint.

5. Toss gently.

6. In a small bowl, blend lemon juice, olive oil, and tamari.

7. Pour dressing over the bulgur and vegetable mix and toss gently.

HEARTY OATMEAL WITH FRUIT AND NUTS

Oatmeal is made from hulled oat grains. It is rich in soluble fiber (especially a unique compound called beta glucan), antioxidants, and B vitamins. Oatmeal can be steel-cut, rolled, or quick/instant.

Home-cooked breakfast oatmeals can be prepared quickly. On a busy morning, they are a great substitute instead of sugar-laden cereals or packages of processed, overly sweetened oatmeal.

Prep Time: 10 minutes
Servings: 2

PHASE 1 2 3

1 cup instant or quick cook oats

2 cups water (or 1 cup of water and 1 cup of milk or a milk substitute--such as, almond, coconut, rice, hemp, and pea)

½ teaspoon Ceylon cinnamon

½ cup fresh or frozen fruit

⅛ cup nuts or seeds (walnuts, cashews, almonds, pecans, pumpkin seeds) or mix in 1 tablespoon of peanut or almond butter

1 tablespoon flax or chia (optional)

A drizzle of sweetener (stevia, 100% maple syrup, honey) to taste (optional)

1 In a medium pot, combine oats and water and bring to a boil. Turn heat down to low and add cinnamon and fruit.

2 Cook until fruit is soft (about 1-2 minutes).

3 Remove from heat and stir in flax or chia if using.

4 Top each bowl with nuts and sweetener if using.

SOME OF OUR FAVORITE COMBINATIONS:

Frozen peaches and blueberries with raw walnuts

Raspberries and pecans

Dried cranberries or cherries with pumpkin seeds

Bananas and peanut butter

EASY BAKED OATMEAL

Blueberry Baked Oatmeal is an easy and hearty breakfast or brunch. Store in refrigerator up to 4 days. Portion and freeze to reheat for a delicious breakfast on the go!

Prep Time: 40 minutes
Servings: 8

PHASE **1** **2** **3**

2 eggs

½ cup unsweetened applesauce

¼ cup honey

1 tablespoon vanilla extract

2 teaspoons cinnamon

½ teaspoon salt

2 teaspoons baking powder

3 cups old fashioned oats

1 cup milk (or unsweetened milk substitute: almond, hemp, rice, soy, pea, coconut)

1 cup fresh or frozen blueberries

Plain greek yogurt, fruit for topping (optional)

1 Preheat oven to 350°F. Oil 9 x 13 pyrex with coconut oil or butter.

2 Whisk eggs, applesauce, brown sugar, and vanilla until smooth.

3 Stir in cinnamon, salt, and baking powder, then add oats and milk.

4 Gently fold in blueberries and spread in prepared pyrex.

5 Bake for 23-35 minutes until oatmeal is browned and not jiggly in the center.

6 Cool slightly before serving.

7 Serve with 100% maple syrup and top with plain yogurt or fruit if desired.

MAKE YOUR OWN SUSHI!

Sushi is a perfect make-your-own-meal. The possibilities are endless. Nori sheets are available at most grocery stores, and you can even buy pickled ginger and wasabi for an authentic sushi experience.

Here are some fun vegetarian ideas to try:

Simply cut each ingredient into long strips for easier rolling.

1 cup of brown rice equals 3 sushi rolls.

PHASE 1 2 3

Sliced avocado

Carrots

Roasted sweet potato

Sliced cucumber

Marinated tofu

Marinated, teriyaki portobello mushrooms

Fresh mango

Steamed asparagus

Baby spinach

Our family favorite is a sweet potato/avocado and mango roll!

BUDDHA BOWL

Buddha bowls or grain bowls are fun and healthy make your own meal. I love hosting a dinner party with all of the fixings laid out beautifully on the table. It is an easy way to cook for a large group and satisfy every palate. For a non-vegetarian option, you can add chicken, beef, lamb or fish.

PHASE **1** **2** **3**

GET CREATIVE:

Mix and Match!

GRAIN:

Choose any grain like cooked quinoa, farro, brown rice as the base..

PROTEIN:

Marinated tofu

Fried egg

Chickpeas

Beans or lentils

Tempeh

Roasted nuts or seeds

Steamed edamame

High quality animal protein

VEGETABLES:

Steam, roast or sautee:

Broccoli

Cauliflower

Sweet potato

Asparagus

Red peppers
(omit for phase 3)

Mushrooms

Kale, collards or spinach

Zucchini

Butternut squash-cubed

FOR CRUNCH:

Sliced or shredded raw carrots, beets or celery

Shredded cabbage (red or green)

Fresh arugula or baby spinach

Cucumber

Toasted sunflower or pumpkin seeds

Sesame seeds

GARNISH WITH:

Easy pickled onions

Pickled jalapenos

Sliced or cubed avocado

Diced fresh parsley or cilantro

Sauces make simple ingredients in the bowl pop with flavor.

Make your own sauces or pick up a few tasty options like teriyaki, carrot ginger or peanut sauce.

CARROT GINGER DRESSING

DRESSING:

⅓ cup extra-virgin olive oil

⅓ cup rice vinegar

2 large carrots, peeled and roughly chopped (about ⅔ cup)

2 tablespoons peeled and roughly chopped fresh ginger

2 tablespoons lime juice

1 tablespoon plus 1 teaspoon honey or maple syrup

1 ½ teaspoons toasted sesame oil

¼ teaspoon salt

1   In a blender or food processor, combine all of the dressing ingredients.

2   Blend until smooth.

3   Drizzle over grain bowl or salad.

TAHINI DRESSING

½ cup tahini

½ teaspoon of salt

2 cloves garlic, finely diced

1 lemon juiced (about ¼ cup)

Approximately ¼ cup water to thin to desired consistency

1   Mix all ingredients except water in a bowl with a whisk or in a blender to combine.

2   Thin with water to desired consistency.

3   Drizzle over salad or grain bowl.

EASY ASIAN PEANUT SAUCE

½ cup of creamy peanut or almond butter

2 teaspoons of 100% maple syrup

2 tablespoons of tamari or soy sauce

1 tablespoon of brown rice vinegar

1 teaspoon of grated ginger root or ½ teaspoon of dry ground ginger

⅛-¼ teaspoon of crushed red pepper (optional)

⅓ cup of water

1 Combine all the ingredients in a small pot or saucepan on low heat on the stove top. Whisk ingredients together until smooth and warm, adding a small amount of water until sauce is desired consistency.

2 If using sauce the next day, simply add more water to thin to the desired consistency.

NUT LOAF

This recipe is a surprisingly delicious and satisfying vegetarian alternative to meatloaf. It is included in this section because it is a great use for any leftover grains.

Prep Time: 20 minutes
Total Cook Time: 40 minutes
Serves: 6

PHASE 1 2 3

2 cups of a finely ground mix of nuts (any combination of raw walnuts, pecans, hazelnuts, sunflower seeds, pumpkin seeds, almonds, cashews) Pulse to grind in a food processor or blender.

1 medium sized onion, chopped

3 cloves of garlic, chopped

3 to 4 ribs of celery, chopped

2 eggs, lightly beaten

1 cup of cooked brown rice, quinoa, farro or other grain

¼ cup of rolled oats

1 tablespoon of tamari

½ teaspoon chopped rosemary

½ teaspoon sage

1 teaspoon caraway seeds

Ketchup

Sea salt to taste

1. In a large pot, saute onions and garlic for about 5 minutes.

2. Add celery, rosemary, sage, and caraway.

3. Remove from heat.

4. Add nut mixture, brown rice or quinoa, eggs, rolled oats, and tamari.

5. Mix thoroughly until all ingredients are well blended.

6. Turn into an oiled loaf pan and spread top with a thin layer of ketchup.

7. Bake at 350°F for 40 minutes.

8. Delicious served with roasted broccoli or roasted sweet potatoes.

ALMOND BUTTER CHIA PUDDING

Although it may seem like a dessert, this pudding makes for an easy to make, nutritious breakfast. While it takes only minutes to prepare, it's best when refrigerated overnight.

PHASE | 1 | 2 | 3

2 bananas, very ripe

1 1/2 cups coconut or almond milk

1/2 cup almond butter

3 tablespoons chia seeds

Fresh berries to garnish-optional

1 Add bananas, coconut or almond milk, and almond butter to a blender and puree.

2 Transfer the mixture into a medium bowl and stir in the chia seeds.

3 Cover and chill in the refrigerator overnight (or for at least four hours).

4 Stir the pudding when ready and then serve.

5 Garnish with fresh berries if desired.

VANILLA CINNAMON CHIA PUDDING

Chia pudding makes a fiber rich breakfast or snack...or enjoy as a satisfying treat to tame your sugar cravings!

PHASE 1 2 3

2 cups non-dairy milk (almond, rice, hemp, pea, soy, coconut)

½ cup chia seeds

2 tablespoons honey or maple syrup

1 teaspoon ground cinnamon, plus more for serving, optional

½ teaspoon vanilla extract

⅛ teaspoon kosher salt

1 Combine the non-dairy milk, chia seeds, honey or maple syrup, cinnamon, vanilla, and salt in a large bowl. Stir until well combined. (Make sure the chia seeds are completely coated in almond milk in order to ensure proper absorption.)

2 Cover and refrigerate for at least 2 hours. Stir before serving, and top with a sprinkle of cinnamon and fruit if desired.

VEGETABLES

Mom was right, eat your vegetables! Vegetables are the ultimate health food, and are the cornerstone of the 21 Day Revival nutrition program for good reason. Vegetables are a rich source of fiber, vitamins, minerals, and complex carbohydrates. They are also packed with cancer-fighting and inflammation-inhibiting phytonutrients.

Vegetables are amazingly versatile and can be eaten raw, roasted, baked, blanched, steamed, sauteed, or grilled as a single-ingredient meal or prepared into any of the more elaborate recipes you'll find in this section.

- **Raw vegetables** are crunchy and sweet. I often put out a plate of veggies with hummus as an appetizer while preparing dinner. Kids (and many adults) are more likely to eat the veggies when they are most hungry. So, I like offering vegetables first! My favorite raw vegetables for crudité are carrots, sugar snap peas, celery, jicama, and broccoli. Fresh salads provide an endless opportunity to get creative and colorful!

- **Roasted:** In our house, we roast a vegetable every night. Our favorites include broccoli, sweet potatoes, brussel sprouts, carrots, and cauliflower. Roasting makes vegetables like sweet potatoes, carrots or butternut squash take on a sweet, almost caramelized flavor. For green vegetables like Brussel sprouts and broccoli, the crispy texture and taste are irresistible. Simply toss vegetables on a baking sheet with olive oil or coconut oil, sprinkle with a little salt, and roast at 400-425°F degrees, shaking the pan as needed to prevent burning.

- **Baked:** Baking vegetables can be a nice alternative to frying. For example, try coating zucchini with breadcrumbs and then baking. I also like baking winter squash, such as butternut squash, acorn squash, and delicata. Baked squash topped with cinnamon and a drizzle of maple syrup is a family favorite!

- **Blanching:** To blanch vegetables, simply boil briefly, and then plunge into cold water to stop the cooking process. This technique is used to make bright, tender-crisp vegetables for Asian salads, sushi, crudités, and many other recipes. I like to use blanched cabbage and carrots to make colorful salads with tasty dressings.

- **Steamed:** Lightly steaming vegetables (prepared with no added fats or oils) is an excellent choice for broccoli, green beans, carrots, or cauliflower. Try steaming covered until vegetables turn a deep, rich color. Remove from heat while there is a little crunch left (or they are fork tender).

- **Sauteed:** This method works well for any single vegetable or a vegetable medley. When sauteeing a combination of vegetables, be mindful of which vegetables take longer to cook and add those to the pan first (cook for a few minutes, and then add the quicker cooking varieties). Most greens like kale, spinach, or collards only need a few minutes to wilt. Heat your pan, add a little olive oil or coconut oil, and toss in your vegetables. Stir frequently.

- **Grilled:** Add some vegetables to your grilling menu. Chop into large pieces and use skewers or kabobs for your summertime grilling. Other options include using a grill basket or placing larger vegetables straight on the grate). Lightly brush vegetables with a marinade to add flavor. Some of my favorite vegetables to grill include onions, corn on the cob, mushrooms, zucchini, crookneck yellow squash, and peppers.

ROASTED BROCCOLI

Broccoli is one of the healthiest vegetables. As a member of the brassicaceae family, it contains potent anti-cancer phytochemicals. In our family, we eat roasted broccoli at least once a week!

PHASE 1 2 3

1 bunch broccoli (about 1 ½ pounds), cut into florets, stems peeled and sliced or diced

2 tablespoons extra-virgin olive oil

Kosher salt

1   Preheat oven to 425°F.

2   Toss the broccoli florets with the olive oil and salt on a baking sheet.

3   For crispier broccoli, keep in single layer while roasting. Shake the tray to crisp each side midway through cooking, roast until the edges are crispy and the stems are crisp tender (about 20 minutes).

BAKED ACORN SQUASH

Butternut, delicata, acorn, or any other winter squash are delicious baked this way. Simply adjust cooking time for smaller squashes.

PHASE `1` `2` `3`

2 acorn squashes

1-2tablespoons Coconut oil or butter

1-2 tablespoons of brown sugar or maple syrup

1 teaspoon cinnamon

1 Preheat oven to 375.

2 Cut squash into quarters without peeling.

3 Brush with coconut oil or butter.

4 Pierce several holes in the flesh.

5 Sprinkle with brown sugar or maple syrup and dust with cinnamon.

6 Bake until tender about 45-50 minutes.

LEMONY GREEN BEANS

Green beans and lemon are delicious combination. I like to cook them until just soft, but still a little snap to them!

PHASE 1 2 3

Green beans, washed and trimmed

1 teaspoon olive oil

1 lemon, juiced

1 tablespoon cornstarch dissolved in ¼ cup of cold water (skip cornstarch for phase 3)

Salt and pepper to taste

1 Heat oil in a pot.

2 Add green beans and stir for 2 minutes.

3 Add cornstarch and water mixture, stirring to thicken.

4 Add lemon juice, salt and pepper to taste.

5 Cover for 1-2 minutes to cook beans until fork tender.

ROASTED CAULIFLOWER WITH TURMERIC

The browned bits of cauliflower are crunchy and delicious! Turmeric adds a bright yellow hue and antiinflammatory action!

PHASE 1 2 3

Cauliflower- cut into 1-inch florets

1-2 tablespoons olive oil

Turmeric 1 teaspoon

Garlic powder 1 teaspoon

Salt ½ teaspoon

1 Preheat oven to 425°F.

2 On a baking tray, toss cauliflower with olive oil, turmeric, garlic and salt.

3 Bake for 20-30 minutes until tender and browned, shaking tray midway to evenly cook all sides.

BAKED POTATO BAR

This is a fun make-your-own meal that is sure to please.

PHASE 1 2 3

White Russet (omit in phase 3)
or Sweet potatoes

Olive oil

Button mushrooms

Broccoli

Shredded cheese
(omit for phase 3)

Plain greek yogurt

Salt and pepper

Garlic powder

1 Preheat oven to 350°F.

2 Wash and dry potatoes.

3 Rub potatoes with olive oil.

4 Pierce potatoes with a fork several times.

5 Bake for 1 - 1 ½ hours until tender.

6 Note: white potatoes can go right on the oven rack, sweet potatoes should be baked on foil or parchment paper as they drip.

FOR TOPPINGS:

1 Broccoli: cut into 1-inch florets and steam until tender, sprinkle with salt.

2 Mushrooms: slice and saute in olive oil and season with garlic powder, salt and pepper.

3 Top each potato with broccoli and mushrooms, add grated cheese and a spoonful of greek yogurt (optional).

BUTTERNUT SQUASH SOUP WITH GINGER AND COCONUT MILK

Creamy butternut squash soup with warming ginger is simple enough for an everyday meal, but fancy enough for company! Especially with fun toppings.

PHASE 1 2 3

3 large butternut squashes

3tablespoons coconut oil or butter

2 medium yellow onions, diced

1-2tablespoons grated ginger

6 cup of vegetable stock

14 ounces of coconut milk

Juice of 1 lime

Salt and pepper to taste

Plain greek yogurt, crispy onions, or toasted pumpkin seeds as garnish- optional

1 Preheat oven to 350°F.

2 Cut squash in half lengthwise and remove seeds, pierce with a fork or knife in a few areas.

3 Brush open halves with coconut oil and place on baking sheet (cut side down) for 1 hour or until tender.

4 Remove from oven and once cool, remove peels and scoop cooked squash into a large bowl and set aside.

5 In a large pot, heat 2 tablespoons of coconut oil or butter. Add onions and ginger and cook over medium heat until soft and golden brown (about 10 minutes). Stir frequently and add a little water to prevent scorching.

6 Add vegetable stock and squash to onions. Simmer on low for 20 minutes.

7 Puree soup until smooth with small batches in the blender or use an immersion blender.

8 Remove soup from heat and stir in coconut milk.

9 Stir in lime juice and salt and pepper to taste.

10 Garnish each bowl of soup with a dollop of plain greek yogurt, crispy onions, or toasted pumpkin seeds.

ROASTED ROOT VEGETABLES

Root vegetables help to detox your liver and nourish your body!

PHASE 1 2 3

1-2 onion, red or yellow, coarsely chopped

1 medium butternut squash, peeled and chopped into 1 to 2-inch cubes

2 Sweet potatoes, peeled and chopped into 1 to 2-inch cubes

4 large beets, peeled and chopped into 1 to 2-inch pieces

2 Parsnips, peeled and chopped into 1 to 2-inch pieces

1 large carrot, peeled and chopped into 1 to 2-inch pieces

5 whole garlic cloves, peeled

2-3tablespoons olive oil

1 ½ teaspoons of sea salt

1   Mix all vegetables together in a large bowl and toss with olive oil and salt.

2   Cover with foil and bake on 375°F for 45 minutes, or until vegetables are all fork tender.

PEA PESTO CROSTINI

This bright green, tangy dip is a perfect party appetizer.

PHASE **1** **2**

1 (10-ounce) package of
frozen peas, thawed

1 garlic clove

½ cup freshly grated
Parmesan cheese

½ teaspoon salt

¼ teaspoon freshly
ground black pepper

⅓ cup olive oil

Juice of one lemon

1 Pulse together in a food processor the peas, garlic, parmesan cheese, salt, and pepper. With the machine running, slowly add olive oil and continue to mix until smooth and well combined. Season with more salt and pepper, if needed.

2 Serve with pita, pita chips, or veggies to dip. Or spread on crostini (brush bread slices with olive oil and grill/broil) and top with halved cherry tomato.

ARTICHOKES WITH LEMON GARLIC SAUCE

Artichokes are an excellent food for liver support, and fun to eat.

(for phase 3, instead of butter, simply drizzle with olive oil, salt, and lemon!)

PHASE 1 2 3

4 large artichokes

1 lemon

4 tablespoons of butter

Salt

Garlic powder

1 Wash and trim stem and sharp tips of each leaf with a knife or sharp scissors.

2 Fill a large stainless-steel or enameled pot with lightly salted water and bring to a boil.

3 Add artichokes and return water to boiling.

4 Reduce heat; simmer, covered, for about 20-30 minutes or until you can easily pull out a leaf from the center of the artichoke.

LEMON GARLIC SAUCE:

1 Melt butter in a small pan or in a pyrex measuring cup in the microwave.

2 Squeeze lemon into melted butter to taste.

3 Add salt and garlic powder.

4 Whisk together and serve as a dipping sauce.

HEARTY VEGETABLE SOUP

This is a very forgiving soup. You can add any/all of your favorite fresh or frozen veggies, and any type of bean or lentil.

PHASE 1 2 3

1-2 tablespoons olive oil

1-2 yellow onions

3-4 garlic cloves

**2 large carrots,
peeled and chopped**

**2 sweet potatoes,
peeled and chopped**

**3 celery stalks,
peeled and chopped**

2 cups of cauliflower, chopped

**1 cup of green beans,
cut into thirds**

4-5 cups of vegetable stock

1 cup of red lentils

½ cup of barley, quinoa or farro

Salt and pepper to taste

Dash of hot sauce- optional

1 Heat oil in a large pot over medium heat.

2 Saute onions for 3-5 minutes, then add garlic and saute for 1 more minute.

3 Add carrots, sweet potato, celery, cauliflower and green beans and stock.

4 Add lentils and grain.

5 Bring to a boil, then cover and simmer on low until vegetables are tender and lentils and grains are soft (about 30 minutes).

6 Season to taste with salt, pepper and hot sauce if desired.

7 Pairs nicely with greek yogurt biscuits.

THAI SALAD WITH GARLIC SESAME DRESSING

This superfood salad is loaded with a rainbow of veggies. Cashews and edamame pack a plant-based protein punch!

PHASE 1 2

SALAD INGREDIENTS:

16 ounces frozen shelled edamame

5 to 6 cups baby kale

3 large carrots

1 red bell pepper

1 yellow bell pepper

1 cup cilantro leaves

3 green onions

3/4 cup cashews

SALAD DRESSING INGREDIENTS

1/3 cup extra virgin olive oil

3 garlic cloves, peeled

3 tablespoons tamari sauce

2 tablespoons water

2 tablespoons white distilled vinegar

2 tablespoons raw honey

1 tablespoon sesame oil

1 tablespoon ginger

Squeeze of lime juice

Salt and pepper to taste

1   For dressing, puree all dressing ingredients in a food processor or high- speed blender until smooth. Add salt and pepper to taste. Set aside.

2   Cook edamame by boiling for 3 to 5 minutes in a pot of boiling water. Drain and allow it to cool.

3   Slice the kale, carrots, peppers, cilantro leaves and green onions into shreds or thin strips.

4   Add cooked edamame and cashews to the vegetables.

5   Toss the kale, carrots, peppers, cilantro, green onions, edamame and cashews together until well combined.

6   Drizzle with the dressing, toss gently several times and serve.

ROASTED BRUSSELS SPROUTS WITH BALSAMIC

Brussels have a bad rap, but if you try them roasted with balsamic, I think you will like them!

PHASE 1 2 3

16 ounces fresh brussels sprouts

1-2 tablespoons olive oil

Salt

1 tablespoon balsamic vinegar

1 Preheat oven to 425°F.

2 Trim stems and half each brussels sprout.

3 Toss with olive oil and salt.

4 Spread evenly on a baking sheet and bake until crispy and browned (about 30 minutes). Shake pan to brown all sides midway through baking.

5 Drizzle with balsamic before serving.

STUFFED MUSHROOMS

Savory stuffed mushrooms are easier to make than you might think. Choose large crimini or baby bella for optimal stuffing capacity.

PHASE **1**

12 whole mushrooms,
about 2-inches in diameter

¼ cup olive oil, divided

¼ cup finely yellow onion

2 cloves garlic, minced

3 tablespoons chopped fresh
parsley, plus more for garnish

½ cup breadcrumbs

½ cup fresh grated
parmesan cheese

½ teaspoon dried oregano

Salt and black pepper, to taste

1 Gently wipe any dirt off the mushrooms with a paper towel or dish towel.

2 Remove the stems from the mushrooms. Cut off and discard the tough tips and finely chop the stems.

3 Heat a skillet over medium heat. Add 2 tablespoons of olive oil.

4 Add the onion, garlic, chopped mushroom stems, and parsley to the skillet with a pinch of salt. Cook until ingredients are softened, stirring occasionally, about 5-7 minutes.

5 In a medium bowl, mix the sautéed mushroom mixture with the breadcrumbs, parmesan cheese, oregano, and salt and pepper to taste.

6 Place the mushrooms in a baking dish. Stuff them with the mixture, pressing down to get as much as possible.

7 Drizzle the remaining two tablespoons of olive oil on top of the stuffed mushrooms.

8 Cover the baking sheet with foil.

9 Bake at 375°F degrees for 20 minutes. Remove foil and bake 10-15 more minutes, until mushrooms are golden and bubbling.

SWEET POTATO CASSEROLE

This delicious sweet potato and pecan casserole is a definite nutritional upgrade from the high sugar, marshmallow-topped variety. It has quickly become our family favorite. We always make a double batch to enjoy as leftovers, as it is usually the first side dish to go! Simplify Thanksgiving by preparing a day in advance, just keep covered and refrigerated, ready to bake for the next day.

Prep Time: 30 minutes
Cook Time: 40 minutes
Serves: 8-9 as a side dish

PHASE 1 2 3

SWEET POTATO MASH:

2 lbs sweet potatoes
(about 3 medium potatoes),
peeled and diced

⅓ cup milk (dairy milk or
unsweetened almond, cashew,
or coconut milk)

3 tablespoons butter or
coconut oil (melted) for phase 3

¼ cup pure maple syrup

1 teaspoon salt

1 teaspoon vanilla

2 eggs

TOPPING:

1 ½ cups pecans (roughly chopped

2 tablespoons butter
or coconut oil (melted)

3 tablespoons pure maple syrup

¾ teaspoon cinnamon

¼ teaspoon salt

SWEET POTATO MASH:

1 Place sweet potatoes in a large pot and cover by 2-3 inches of water.

2 Bring to a boil over medium-high heat.

3 Boil until completely tender.

4 Drain sweet potatoes.

5 Transfer potatoes to a large mixing bowl and add milk, butter/oil, syrup, salt, vanilla, and egg.

6 Mash or use immersion blender to mix until smooth.

7 Pour mash into an oiled 8 × 8 or 2-quart baking dish and smooth the surface.

8 When ready to bake, preheat the oven to 375°F degrees and make the topping.

TOPPING:

1 In a medium bowl, combine pecans, butter/oil, syrup, cinnamon, and salt.

2 Sprinkle over the sweet potato mash.

3 Cover the dish with foil and bake 20 minutes at 375°F degrees.

4 Remove foil and bake another 20-25 minutes. If pecans begin to brown too quickly, simply cover with foil again.

AVOCADO TOAST

This breakfast is a staple in our house!

PHASE 1

Whole grain bread

Neufchatel, cream cheese or hummus

1 ripe avocado, sliced

Sea salt

Everything bagel seasoning (you can buy premade or make your own with sesame seeds, salt, dehydrated garlic, dehydrated onion, black sesame seeds and poppy seeds)

Smoked salmon or fried egg (optional)

1 Toast the bread.

2 Spread lightly with neufchatel, cream cheese, or hummus.

3 Arrange sliced avocado on top and sprinkle with everything seasoning or simply sea salt.

4 Add smoked salmon or a fried or hard boiled egg for additional protein (if desired).

GNOCCHI WITH SUMMER SQUASH

This easy recipe can be made with any vegetable variation and is quick to prepare.

PHASE 1

1-2 tablespoons olive oil

1 yellow onion, diced

3 cloves of garlic, minced

2-3 medium zucchini or crookneck yellow squash, sliced into thin semi circles

1 package of gnocchi

Salt and pepper

Red pepper flakes

Parmesan cheese (optional)

1 Bring a pot of salted water to a boil and cook gnocchi as directed on package, and set aside.

2 Heat oil in a skillet over medium heat.

3 Add onions, saute until translucent (about 5 minutes).

4 Add garlic and saute for 2 more minutes.

5 Add squash and saute until tender.

6 Season with salt, pepper, and red pepper flakes to taste.

7 Serve over gnocchi sprinkled with parmesan cheese.

BEANS, LENTILS, AND CHICKPEAS

What do green beans, peas, kidney beans, soybeans, peanuts, chickpeas, and lentils have in common? They are all part of the Fabaceae or Leguminosae plant family, a species that scientists believed may have originated in Africa as many as 4 million years ago!

Legumes are among the most versatile, healthy, and delicious foods you can eat, and there are almost 20,000 varieties of legumes that have been cultivated and consumed since ancient times.

Today, studies show that eating legumes regularly can help you prevent and treat a wide variety of health issues; including constipation, heart disease, type 2 diabetes, cancer, high cholesterol, and obesity. Here's a quick summary of the best evidence we have regarding how legumes can benefit your health:

How Legumes Benefit Your Health

- Legumes are an excellent source of fiber, which helps keep your bowels regular.

- Fiber-rich legumes can help lower your cholesterol while helping to keep your blood glucose levels in check.

- They are a great alternative to meat because they are an excellent source of nutrients and protein (but without the cholesterol and saturated fat found in animal proteins).

- Legumes are an excellent source of phytonutrients, antioxidants, and minerals. Some of the beneficial compounds in legumes include iron, B vitamins, as well as zinc, magnesium, and potassium.

- Legumes are a nutrient dense food, which means you can get a wide variety of beneficial phytonutrients *without* consuming a lot of calories.

- Studies indicate that eating heart-healthy legumes can significantly lower your risk for cardiovascular disease.

Canned vs. Dried Beans

The beans recipes in this cookbook can be made with canned beans or dried beans that you soak and cook yourself. I prefer the taste and texture of dried beans cooked at home, but it can be hard to remember to soak the beans and cook for each recipe. We always have canned beans as a staple in our pantry, and often use canned beans for a quick protein in recipes. If you use canned beans, drain and rinse to remove excess sodium.

If you prefer to cook dried beans yourself, here's how it's done:

- Soak: 6-8 hours or overnight.
- Cover beans with water by about 2-inches.
- Drain the soaking water.
- Add fresh water (twice as much as dried beans). For example, if you have 1 cup of dried beans, add 2 cups of fresh water.
- For stovetop simmering: 45-60 minutes on a low heat.
- For pressure cooking: bring heat up to high, allow pressure gauge to rise, then reduce heat (though still hot enough for the gauge to stay up) and cook for about 45 minutes.
- Salt after cooking.

Beans are done when they are tender enough to mash easily in your mouth with your tongue.

Useful conversions for dry versus canned beans:

- 1 cup of dry beans yields approximately 3 cups of cooked beans.
- A 15 ounce can = about 1 ½ cups of beans.
- If a recipe calls for 1 cup of dried beans, you can use two 15-ounce cans.
- If a recipe calls for one 15-ounce can, you can cook a ¾ cup of dried beans.

ONE-POT TUSCAN WHITE BEAN STEW

This easy Mediterranean one-pot meal is hearty and delicious!

Cook Time: 40 minutes
Serves: 4-6

PHASE 1 2

2 tablespoons of
extra virgin olive oil

4 garlic cloves, thinly sliced

¼ teaspoon red pepper flakes

1 can (14.5-ounce) diced tomatoes

4 cups vegetable broth

1 teaspoon kosher salt

½ teaspoon ground black pepper

1 medium butternut squash peeled
and cubed (about 2 cups)

2 celery stalks, chopped

1 can (15-ounce)
white beans, drained

1 bunch lacinato kale or baby
spinach, stems removed,
roughly chopped

Toasted bread and shaved
vegetarian parmesan to serve
(optional)

1 Heat olive oil in a large pot over medium heat.

2 Add onion, garlic and red pepper flakes and cook until fragrant (about 2 minutes).

3 Add celery and saute for 2 minutes.

4 Add diced tomatoes (with juice) and continue cooking for an additional 2 minutes.

5 Add vegetable broth, butternut squash, salt, and pepper and simmer until butternut squash is fork tender (about 15 minutes).

6 Add white beans and kale or spinach and stir to wilt.

7 Optional: Serve with toasted bread and garnish with parmesan cheese except during phase 2-3.

SWEET POTATO BLACK BEAN BURRITO

A friend brought me these burritos after the birth of my second daughter. I called them "the burritos of salvation" when they arrived at the end of a particularly exhausting day. Nothing ever tasted so good! The flavors are surprisingly complex and they heat up well for a lunch you will look forward to!

Prep Time: 45 minutes
Cook Time: 25-30 minutes
Serves: 6

PHASE 1

6 cups of peeled and cubed sweet potatoes

2 cups of chopped onions

3 cloves of garlic minced

2 tablespoons of olive oil

1 tablespoon of garam masala

1 tablespoon of cumin

2 (15-ounce) cans of black beans, drained and rinsed

2 tablespoons of lemon juice

½ cup of cilantro chopped

1 small jalapeno, seeded and diced

Salt to taste

6 10-inch tortillas

Salsa

Shredded cheddar cheese

1   Steam sweet potatoes in covered saucepan until tender and set aside.

2   In a large pot, cook onions, garlic, jalapeno in oil until soft (about 10 minutes).

3   Add garam masala and cumin to the onion mixture, and add cooked sweet potatoes.

4   Combine sweet potatoes, onion mixture and beans. Chunky texture is fine, but If you prefer a smooth consistency, you can blend with immersion blender or food processor.

5   Add lemon juice, cilantro and salt to taste.

6   Lightly oil a 9 x 13 pyrex, place about ¾ cup of filling to each tortilla and roll into burrito. Place each burrito in pyrex. Cover with salsa and sprinkle with cheese if desired.

7   Bake for 25-30 minutes.

THREE SISTERS STEW

In Native American mythology, squash, corn, and beans are known as the "three sisters." This hearty harvest stew is perfect for fall. It combines warming spices like cinnamon and chili powder with pinto beans, seasonal butternut squash, and corn for a satisfying, fiber rich dinner. Leftovers heat up nicely for an easy hot lunch.

Cook Time: 30 minutes
Serves: 6-8

PHASE 1 2

2 cups of pinto beans
(drained and rinsed)

2-3 cups vegetable or
chicken stock or water

2 teaspoons ground cumin

1 tablespoon olive oil or ghee

1 medium onion, chopped

2 teaspoons sea salt

3 cloves garlic, minced

2 teaspoons dry oregano

½ teaspoon cinnamon

1 teaspoon chili powder

2-3 cups butternut squash,
peeled and cut into 1-inch chunks

1 can (14-ounce) of
diced tomatoes

1 ½ cups fresh or
frozen corn kernels

½ cup grated cheese
(optional garnish)

1. Heat a 4-quart pot, add oil. Add onion, salt and garlic; sauté until onion is soft (5 minutes).

2. Add cumin, oregano, cinnamon and chili powder and cook for about 30 seconds.

3. Add 1-2 cups of stock or water.

4. Add squash and tomatoes, bring to a simmer and cook until the squash is soft (about 20 minutes).

5. Add beans and corn; simmer until corn is tender.

6. Add remaining stock or water to desired thickness.

7. Serve with a chunk of whole grain bread or over a bed of brown rice.

8. Top with a sprinkle of grated cheese if desired.

BLACK BEAN AND MANGO SALAD

This colorful salad is perfect for a festive party appetizer or for use as a delicious plant-based, antioxidant-rich protein alternative to chicken to top your salad or grain!

PHASE 1 2

15.8 oz can black beans, drained and rinsed

1 cup sweet red, orange or yellow bell pepper, diced

6 green onions, thinly sliced

1 jalapeno pepper, seeded and minced

¼ cup cilantro leaves, chopped

¼ cup fresh lime juice

1 tablespoon olive oil

¼ teaspoon garlic powder

¼ teaspoon cumin powder

2 cups mango, diced

Sea salt (or kosher salt) to taste

Pumpkin seeds or chunks of avocado (optional)

1 In a large bowl, combine drained and rinsed black beans, diced bell peppers, green onions, minced jalapeno pepper, and fresh cilantro.

2 In a separate small bowl, whisk together olive oil, lime juice, garlic and cumin powders.

3 Pour olive oil, lime juice and spice mixture over the bean mix, and gently toss together until well combined.

4 Once ingredients are mixed, carefully fold in diced mango and season lightly with sea salt.

5 Sprinkle with toasted pumpkin seeds or chunks of avocado (optional).

6 Serve with tortilla chips, add a scoop to jazz up your salad or serve over quinoa!

CRISPY BUTTER BEANS AND BROCCOLI

Crispy butter beans are a fun to serve over pasta, but If you are in a hurry, simply add rinsed beans to the mix and skip the crisping part! For phase 2, simply serve over brown rice or quinoa.

Cook time: 35 minutes
Serves: 4

PHASE 1 2

2 cans butter beans,
drained and rinsed

Olive oil

Salt and pepper to taste

Red chile flakes

1 ½ pounds broccoli cut
into small florets

4 garlic cloves, diced

1 lemon

8 ounces whole grain spaghetti

1. Add salt to a large pot of water and bring to a boil. Cook pasta until tender, but not mushy. Drain in colander and set aside.

2. Drain and rinse the butter beans in a colander, and then spread them out on a paper towel to dry.

3. Add 2 tablespoons oil to a large skillet over medium-high heat.

4. When hot, add the beans and shake the pan gently to spread them into a single layer. Sprinkle with salt and pepper and cook, stirring occasionally until crisp (about 5-10 minutes).

5. Add a pinch of chile flakes (Taste and adjust the seasoning, adding more chile flakes to taste).

6. Remove the pan from the heat and transfer the beans to a plate (there's no need to clean the pan, just set aside.

7. Return skillet to medium heat and add 2 tablespoons of oil. Saute garlic for 1-2 minutes and then add broccoli. Cover and cook, stirring occasionally until broccoli is tender. Add a little water if needed to avoid scorching.

8. Combine pasta, beans and broccoli mixture in the pan. Add salt and pepper to taste.

9. Serve with a lemon wedge to add a zing of flavor!

WEST AFRICAN PEANUT SOUP WITH CHICKPEAS

This West African peanut soup recipe is a creamy and comforting, spicy vegan soup. Made with a simple combination of peanut butter, tomato paste, and collard greens, this soup comes together quickly and can be a great weeknight meal. If you love spicy flavors like me, don't hesitate to use liberal amounts of ginger and garlic.

Cook Time: 45 minutes
Serves: 4

PHASE 1 2

6 cups vegetable broth

1 medium red onion, chopped

2 medium sweet potatoes, peeled and chopped into 1-inch cubes

2 tablespoons peeled and minced fresh ginger

4 cloves garlic, minced

1 teaspoon salt

1 can of chickpeas, drained and rinsed

1 bunch collard greens (or kale), ribs removed and leaves chopped into 1-inch strips

¾ cup unsalted peanut butter (chunky or smooth)

½ cup tomato paste

Hot sauce, like sriracha or tabasco

¼ cup roughly chopped peanuts, for garnish

1 Saute onions, ginger, garlic and salt in large pot for 10 minutes. Add broth and bring to a boil. Add sweet potatoes and cook on medium-low heat until sweet potatoes are tender (about 20 minutes).

2 In a medium-sized, heat-safe mixing bowl, combine the peanut butter and tomato paste, then transfer 1 to 2 cups of the hot broth to the bowl. Whisk the mixture together until smooth, then pour the peanut mixture back into the soup and mix well. Stir in chickpeas and collard greens.

3 Simmer for about 15 minutes on medium-low heat, stirring often.

4 Optional: add hot sauce to taste and serve over cooked brown rice.

5 Garnish with a sprinkle of chopped peanuts.

MEXICAN BEAN AND POLENTA CASSEROLE

Take Mexican night to a new level with this polenta casserole. It is pretty easy to make and looks lovely when served.

Serves: 8

PHASE **1** 2

1-2 teaspoons olive oil

2 cloves of garlic

1 onion, diced

½ teaspoon salt

1 cup chopped zucchini

2 teaspoons ground cumin

1 teaspoon oregano

½ cup tomato sauce

¼ cup of water

3 cups of water

1 teaspoon salt

1 tablespoon of olive oil or butter

1 cup of polenta

1 tablespoon of parmesan cheese (optional)

2 cans of pinto beans, drained and rinsed

FOR THE BEAN AND VEGETABLE MIXTURE:

1 Heat olive oil in a large pot or skillet.

2 Saute onions, garlic and salt until soft.

3 Add zucchini, cumin oregano and saute for 5 more minutes.

4 Add beans and tomato sauce to the zucchini/onion mixture with ¼ cup of water to prevent scorching. Spread mixture across bottom of oiled casserole dish.

FOR THE POLENTA:

1 In a separate pot, bring 3 cups of water to a boil.

2 Add salt and oil/butter.

3 Slowly add polenta, stir continuously with a whisk.

4 Lower heat and stir until mixture has thickened to be able to hold a spoon upright.

5 Spread thickened polenta over the bean and vegetable mixture.

6 Sprinkle parmesan on top if desired.

7 Bake covered for 25 minutes at 350°F, then 5 more minutes uncovered at 400°F.

RED LENTIL SOUP WITH COCONUT MILK AND LIME

Coconut milk makes this lentil soup creamy and filling, and I love the addition of lime before serving.

Cook Time: 30 minutes
Serves: 4

PHASE

2 tablespoons olive oil

2 small yellow onion, diced

1 tablespoon of fresh ginger, peeled and minced

1 teaspoon ground cumin

½ teaspoon ground coriander

4 cloves of garlic, minced

3-4 cups of vegetable stock

1 cup of red lentils, rinsed

1 cup of coconut milk

½ jalapeno, seeded and finely minced (optional)

3 tablespoons of fresh basil, chopped

2-3 tablespoons of fresh lime juice

Salt to taste

Dollop of plain greek yogurt to garnish (optional).

1   Heat oil in a large pot.

2   Saute onion about 5-10 minutes
    over medium heat.

3   Add ginger, cumin, coriander
    and garlic. Stir for 1-2 minutes.

4   Add vegetable stock, lentils, and
    jalapeno (if using).

5   Bring to light boil and then
    cover and reduce heat to a
    simmer until lentils are tender,
    about 15-20 minutes.

6   Add coconut milk and allow
    soup to cool slightly before
    puree in a food processor or
    with an immersion blender until
    smooth.

7   Reheat to serving temperature.

8   Stir in basil and lime juice
    before serving. Or serve each
    bowl with a section of lime to
    squeeze. Salt to taste.

9   Top with a dollop of plain greek
    yogurt (optional).

RED BEAN AND QUINOA CHILI

Whole grain quinoa and red beans are a perfect nutritional combo. This warming, plant-based chili is a tasty and satisfying one-pot meal. Add a salad for an easy and well-balanced dinner.

Time: 45 minutes
Serves: 4-6

PHASE

2 cans (15-ounces each) of kidney beans, drained and rinsed

1 teaspoon cumin

1 tablespoon olive oil

1 medium onion, chopped

1-2 teaspoons sea salt

2 garlic cloves, minced

1 large red pepper, chopped

1 teaspoon dried oregano

1/4 teaspoon cinnamon

1/8 teaspoon cayenne

2/3 cup quinoa, rinsed in warm water and drained (not cooked)

1 cup frozen corn

1 cup organic tomato sauce

1 cup water

1 bunch of kale or spinach, chopped

Grated cheddar cheese (optional)

1   Drain and rinse beans.

2   Heat oil in a skillet on medium heat.

3   Add onion, 1 teaspoon of salt, garlic, red pepper, cumin, oregano, cinnamon, and cayenne. Saute for 5-10 minutes.

4   Add rinsed quinoa and stir in. Add corn, tomato sauce and water to onion/quinoa mixture. Simmer together 20 minutes.

5   Add cooked beans.

6   Add kale or spinach and simmer until greens are wilted.

7   Simmer for another 5-10 minutes, salt and pepper to taste .

8   Top each bowl with a sprinkle of grated cheese (if desired).

BUTTER BEANS WITH PESTO, ARTICHOKE HEARTS AND SUNDRIED TOMATOES

This dish comes together quickly for a weeknight dinner with serious flavor.

Serve over pasta (phase 1) or a whole grain.

Serves: 4-6

PHASE | 1 | 2

1 yellow onion, chopped

2-3 cloves of garlic, minced

1 large carrot, peeled and chopped

2 celery stalks, chopped

2 cans of butter beans, drained and rinsed

1 can of artichoke hearts, quartered or halved

¼ cup of sundried tomatoes in oil, diced

1 lemon, juiced

3-4 tablespoons of prepared pesto (our favorite brand is costco)

1   Saute onions and garlic until soft (about 5-10 minutes).

2   Add carrots and celery and saute for 5-10 more minutes.

3   Add beans, artichoke hearts, and sundried tomatoes.

4   Add lemon juice, stir carefully to combine without making the ingredients mushy.

5   Salt and pepper to taste.

6   Add prepared pesto to taste.

ROASTED SWEET POTATO AND CHICKPEA SALAD

This fancy salad is packed with flavor and easy to make. (skip the feta for phase 3)

Serves: 4

PHASE 1 2 3

2 medium sweet potatoes, cut into ½-inch thick half-rounds, skin-on

1 cup extra virgin olive oil, divided

¾ teaspoon kosher salt, divided

¼ teaspoon ground black pepper

1 can (15-ounce) chickpeas, drained

¼ teaspoon chili powder

¼ cup balsamic vinegar

4 cups baby arugula

½ cup crumbled feta

½ cup pomegranate seeds

¼ cup roughly chopped mint

1 Preheat oven to 400°F.

2 Toss sweet potato slices with 2 tablespoons olive oil, ½ teaspoon salt, and ¼ teaspoon pepper. Place on one half of a sheet tray divided with tin foil.

3 Toss chickpeas with 2 tablespoons of olive oil, ¼ teaspoon salt, and ¼ teaspoon chili powder and place on the other half of sheet tray.

4 Place sheet tray in oven and bake until potatoes are tender and chickpeas are golden (about 20 minutes).

5 Cool completely and set aside.

BALSAMIC VINAIGRETTE:

1 Combine remaining ¾ cup olive oil with balsamic vinegar and seasonings to taste with salt and pepper (if making ahead of time, give it a stir before serving).

2 In a large bowl, combine arugula, feta, pomegranate seeds, mint, roasted sweet potatoes, and chickpeas.

3 Dress with balsamic vinaigrette to taste and serve immediately.

CHANA MASALA

Enjoy this Indian classic dish at home. Jalapeno or serrano pepper add some spiciness, but you prefer flavor without heat, simply omit or decrease the amount to taste.

PHASE **1** **2**

½ small red onion, finely chopped

2 tablespoons lemon juice

½ teaspoon salt

1 tablespoon olive oil

2 medium onions, chopped

3 cloves garlic, minced

2 teaspoons grated fresh ginger

1 chili pepper jalapeno or serrano, de-seeded and minced

1 tablespoon ground coriander

2 teaspoons ground cumin

1 teaspoon ground turmeric

2 teaspoons ground cumin seeds

1 teaspoon paprika

1 ½ teaspoon garam masala

2 cups tomatoes, chopped small or 1 can (15-ounce) of whole tomatoes with their juices, chopped small

⅔ cup water

2 (15-ounce) cans chickpeas, drained and rinsed

1   Add finely chopped red onion to lemon juice and salt and set aside.

2   Heat oil in a large skillet. Add onion, garlic, ginger and pepper and sauté over medium heat until browned (about 5-8 minutes).

3   Turn heat down to medium-low and add the coriander, cumin, turmeric, cumin, paprika and garam masala.

4   Cook onion mixture with spices for a minute or two, then add the tomatoes and any accumulated juices, scraping up any bits that have stuck to the pan.

5   Add the water and chickpeas. Simmer uncovered for 10-15 minutes.

6   Stir in red onions, salt and lemon juice mixture before serving.

7   Serve over rice or with warmed naan bread (phase 1).

WHITE BEAN AND KALE MINESTRONE

Cannellini beans or white beans are a popular ingredient in Tuscan cooking. They have a creamy texture and mild flavor that pairs well with powerhouse greens like kale or spinach. Fresh lemon makes this delicious soup burst with flavor.

Servings: 4

PHASE 1 2

- 1 ½ - 2 cups finely chopped kale
- 1 tablespoon extra virgin olive oil
- 2 large cloves of garlic
- 3 cups cooked white beans or cannellini
- 2 ½ cups vegetable stock
- 1 tablespoon tomato paste
- 4-6 sage leaves
- 1 teaspoon sea salt
- Freshly ground black pepper
- 1 tablespoon fresh lemon juice
- Optional: Freshly grated parmesan cheese

1 Wash kale and remove the stems from the leaves. Rollup kale leaves and cut into thin ribbons. Set aside.

2 In a 4-quart soup pot, heat olive oil and sauté the garlic briefly over medium heat. Add about half of the cooked beans and part of the stock. Puree the rest of the beans and stock in the blender along with the tomato paste and sage. Stir the pureed beans into the soup. Add salt and pepper to taste.

3 Mix the kale into the soup and simmer until kale has wilted (about 10 minutes).

4 Add the lemon juice and enough water to make the soup a desirable thick consistency. Taste for salt and pepper and adjust seasonings accordingly.

5 Serve the soup topped with grated parmesan cheese (optional).

LEMONY CHICKPEAS

Chickpeas or garbanzo beans are an easy plant-based protein to include in your diet. Whether you are a vegetarian or just trying to be heart-healthy, this recipe is quick, flavorful and easy to make. Garlic and onions boost the immune system and the carrots and yellow squash are packed with beta carotene. Turmeric decreases inflammation and adds a rich yellow hue to this tasty dish.

PHASE `1` `2` `3`

15 oz chickpeas- drained and rinsed

1 tablespoon olive oil to saute onions

1 medium onion, chopped

2 cloves garlic, minced, or ½ teaspoon of garlic powder

2 large carrots, peeled and sliced

1 medium yellow squash, sliced

½ teaspoon turmeric powder

1-2 lemons, juiced

Salt and pepper to taste

Optional: Serve over brown rice or quinoa

1 Saute onions in olive oil until golden brown, add garlic.

2 Add sliced carrots and yellow squash.

3 Continue cooking for about 10 minutes until vegetables are soft.

4 Add rinsed chickpeas, then stir in turmeric, salt, pepper, and the juice of 1-2 lemons.

5 Serve over brown rice or quinoa.

SWEET AND SPICY BARBEQUE BEANS

This recipe is a definite upgrade from overly sweet, mushy barbeque baked beans in a can. These BBQ beans have serious flavor and pair well with cornbread as a main dish.

Serves: 4

PHASE | 1 | 2

2 cans of pinto beans, drained and rinsed

6 ounces tomato paste

2 tablespoons apple cider vinegar

⅓ cup molasses

⅓ cup 100% maple syrup

1 teaspoon sea salt

¼ teaspoon black pepper

1-2 canned chipotle peppers

1 teaspoon dijon mustard

¼ teaspoon ground cloves

¾ cup of water

1 Combine tomato paste, vinegar, molasses, maple syrup, sea salt, pepper, chipotle, mustard, cloves and water in a blender and pulse until smooth.

2 In a large saucepan, pour sauce over beans and simmer until they are heated. Allow beans to marinate in the sauce for at least 15 minutes to absorb the flavor.

3 Delicious served with cornbread and a side green vegetable.

QUESADILLAS (SIMPLE AND FANCY)

Quesadillas are our family's version of fast food. A quick, delicious meal that can be made in minutes before soccer practice or dance.

PHASE 1

Whole wheat or corn tortilla

Beans: refried, black beans, white beans, leftover chicken, or beef

Grated cheese: cheddar or Monterey Jack

Optional: salsa, sliced avocado

1 Heat pan with a little olive oil or butter.

2 Spread or sprinkle beans onto tortilla, add chicken or meat if using.

3 Sprinkle with cheese.

4 Fold tortilla to form a half circle.

5 Flip once to brown each side.

6 Serve with salsa or sliced avocado.

VARIATIONS:

- Make a plain cheese quesadilla and have beans on the side.

- Use leftover sweet potato as part of the filling instead of cheese for dairy free quesadilla.

- Customize your quesadilla by adding thinly sliced raw or pickled red onions, sauteed mushrooms, thawed frozen corn kernels, or any other filling.

SPICY TORTILLA SOUP

This vegetarian version of classic tortilla soup is packed with flavor!

PHASE 1

2 tablespoons of olive oil

1 large yellow onion, chopped

4 cloves of garlic, diced

1 jalapeno, remove seeds, finely chop (use half if you prefer less spicy!)

1 ½ teaspoon chile powder

2 canned chipotles in adobo sauce, finely chopped (found in mexican section of grocery store) Use less if you prefer less spicy

1 can (28-ounce) of crushed tomatoes

4 cups of vegetable broth

2 cups of corn kernels (fresh or frozen)

2 cans (15-ounce) of black beans, drained and rinsed

2 avocados, diced

½ cup fresh cilantro, diced for garnish

Lime wedges (optional)

FOR THE TORTILLA STRIPS:

Olive oil

8 small corn tortillas cut into ¼-inch strips

Kosher salt

1 Heat oil in a large pot, add onion, garlic and jalapeno. Cook until onion is translucent (about 7 minutes), stirring occasionally.

2 Add chile powder, chipotles, black beans, and tomatoes and cook for 5 minutes.

3 Add vegetable broth, corn and simmer on a low heat to meld the flavors.

4 Salt and pepper to taste.

FOR THE TORTILLA STRIPS:

1 Toss tortilla strips with olive oil and salt.

2 Spread onto a baking sheet and bake at 350°F until crisp and lightly browned (about 10-15 minutes), but check frequently to avoid burning.

TO ASSEMBLE THE BOWLS:

Divide tortilla strips on the bottom of each bowl, ladle soup into each bowl and garnish with avocado, cilantro and a squeeze of lime if desired.

PANNA COTTA

You can use traditional escarole or spinach to make this Italian classic.

PHASE 1

1 large head of escarole or 2 bunches of spinach, rinsed and chopped

1 large yellow onion, chopped

2-3 cloves of garlic, minced

3 tablespoons of olive oil

1 cup of cooked cannellini beans

½ cup vegetable broth

Salt and pepper

2-3 cups of italian or sourdough bread, cubed

½ cup parmesan cheese

1   Preheat oven to 350°F.

2   Saute onions and garlic in olive oil until soft.

3   If using fresh escarole, remove core, chop leaves roughly and boil in salted water until tender, then add to onions.

4   If using spinach, no need to boil, simply add spinach to onions and stir until wilted.

5   Add beans and ½ cup of vegetable broth to make a slightly soupy mixture.

6   Add salt and pepper to taste.

7   In a lightly oiled 9 x 13 baking dish, spread ½ of the cubed bread to cover the bottom.

8   Spoon onions, greens and bean mixture over bread.

9   Sprinkle with ¼ cup parmesan cheese.

10   Cover with top layer of cubed bread and sprinkle generously with parmesan cheese.

11   Bake for 20-30 minutes until cheese is slightly browned.

ROASTED CHICKPEAS

These tasty chickpeas make a great high-protein, high-fiber snack. You can also add them to a grain bowl or salad!

PHASE **1** 2 3

1 can (15-ounce) chickpeas (garbanzo beans), drained

1-2 tablespoons olive oil

Salt

garlic powder

Turmeric

Paprika

Ginger

Cayenne (optional)

1 Preheat oven to 450°F degrees.

2 Blot chickpeas with a paper towel to dry them.

3 In a bowl, toss chickpeas with olive oil, and season to taste with salt, garlic powder, paprika, ginger, turmeric, and cayenne pepper, if using.

4 Spread on a baking sheet, and bake for 30-40 minutes, until browned and crunchy. Watch carefully the last few minutes to avoid burning.

SOY: TOFU, MISO, TEMPEH

It's hard to believe that the humble soybean has caused so much controversy! Patients come into my office confused as to whether soy is a healthy choice, or a high-risk food. There have been a lot of conflicting opinions about soy in the past few years. Some experts believe it's an essential alternative to animal-based protein, while others recommend avoiding soy completely.

Soy has been consumed as a traditional food in Asian cultures for centuries. It has been associated with many health benefits such as the relief of menopausal symptoms, lower rates of heart disease, improved cholesterol, a decreased risk for breast cancer, and higher bone density.

In the 21 Day Revival program and in this cookbook, soy is included but with some important exceptions.

Soy To Avoid:

Genetically modified (GMO) soybeans, soy-based supplements, and highly-processed soy products do not have the same health benefits as traditional soy foods. These "frankensoy" foods like fake meat and dairy products (soy milk, soy yogurt, soy bacon, soy bologna, soy chicken, soy cheese, soy and soy sausage) are high tech processed foods that have never been part of any traditional diet. As with other food types, seeking out traditional soy products (whole foods varieties, not processed) is the healthiest and safest way to incorporate soy into your diet.

What Are the Best Types of Soy?

The soy-based recipes included in this cookbook make use of traditional soy foods only. To make these recipes, you should choose organic, non-GMO traditional soy foods like:

- Tofu
- Tempeh
- Edamame
- Miso

Enjoy Soy in Moderation:

Two to three servings per week are optimal for most people.

As with any food, it is possible to have a soy allergy or digestive symptoms after eating soy. If you are allergic or do not tolerate soy, choose other plant-based foods like chickpeas, beans, lentils, and flax to incorporate into your healthy diet.

SWEET POTATO, CAULIFLOWER, AND TOFU FAJITA

This may seem like an odd combination, but trust me...this vegan fajita is tasty and filling!

For phase two and three, omit tortillas and serve over rice.

PHASE **1** **2** **3**

1 tablespoon of coconut or olive oil

2-3 medium sized sweet potatoes, thinly sliced into ½-inch pieces

½ head cauliflower, thinly sliced into 1-inch pieces

1 large onion, coarsely chopped

1 package of firm tofu, cut into 1-inch cubes

¼-½ cup of teriyaki sauce (our favorite is Soy Vay*)

Juice from 1 lime

Water as necessary to prevent scorching

Whole wheat or corn tortillas

Salsa, shredded cheese, fresh avocado slices as optional toppings

1 In a large pot, saute onions for 5-7 minutes.

2 Add sweet potatoes, cauliflower, teriyaki sauce and lime juice. Stir frequently to prevent scorching. Add small amount of water if needed. Cook until veggies are tender. Add the tofu and cover and simmer on low for 5 minutes.

3 Spoon filling onto tortillas or over rice and serve with salsa, cheese (optional) and sliced avocado for topping.

* Soy Vay Teriyaki is not a gluten-free option - if you have gluten sensitivity substitute with another gluten-free option like Kikkoman Teriyaki.

HEARTY MISO SOUP

Miso is a true superfood. This recipe uses a simple miso broth as a base of a hearty, warming meal. The recipe is very forgiving, and welcomes additions or substitutions to suit your personal preferences.

PHASE `1` `2` `3`

5 cups water

2 tablespoons Olive oil

1 large onion, chopped

3-4 large carrots, sliced on the diagonal

2 cups shiitake mushrooms, sliced (any other mushroom variety will do)

2-3 stalks celery, sliced

3 cups greens (bok choy or spinach)

1 pound extra firm tofu, cut into 1-inch cubes

4-5 cloves garlic, minced

3 tablespoons fresh ginger, minced (1 tablespoon powdered ginger works too)

¼ cup white miso, dissolved in broth

Soy sauce to taste

1tablespoon of toasted sesame oil, optional

Cooked soba or rice noodles (optional) omit for phase 2 and 3

2-3 scallions, chopped as garnish (optional)

1 In a large pot, saute the onion in olive oil until translucent.

2 Once the onions are soft, add the garlic and ginger and add the rest of the vegetables (except for the greens) one at a time.

3 Keep stirring to prevent charring and add a little broth if necessary to keep it moist.

4 As the vegetables begin to soften, add the liquid and bring to a boil. Turn the heat down to low and add all remaining ingredients except the miso, kale, and noodles.

5 Cover and simmer on low for 10-15 minutes, or until the carrots are soft. Turn off the heat and add the tofu and the greens, stirring until the greens wilt.

6 In a separate bowl, mix the miso paste with enough broth to dissolve, then add back into the pot.

7 Add 1 tablespoon of toasted sesame oil.

8 Remove from heat and add the cooked noodles (optional).

9 Add soy sauce to taste and garnish with sliced scallions.

HAWAIIAN BARBEQUE TOFU BOWL

Looking for a flavorful plant-based meal? This mouthwatering, tropical tofu bowl is packed with flavor, fiber, and color! Omit red peppers for phase 3.

Prep Time: 35 minutes
Cook Time: 20 minutes
Serves: 4 people

PHASE   1   2   3

1 package (14-ounce)
extra firm tofu

2 cups quinoa, cooked

½ cup barbecue sauce,
plus more for topping

Olive oil (or coconut oil) for
sauteing vegetables and tofu

1 red pepper, thinly sliced

1 zucchini, thinly sliced

½ red onion, thinly sliced

½ pineapple, cored and sliced
(or 2 mangoes, sliced)

OPTIONAL TOPPING:

Coconut flakes, unsweetened

Cilantro, chopped

Avocado, cubed

1 Drain the tofu. Place tofu on a plate and put a heavy object (like a pot) on top of the tofu to press the water out. Let the tofu drain for 20-30 minutes, then pour off the liquid.

2 Slice the drained tofu into thin ½-inch chunks. Place in a medium bowl, then add barbecue sauce and marinate for 10 minutes.

3 In a skillet over medium heat, warm up a little oil. Add red peppers and zucchini, then stir. Cook for 5-7 minutes until vegetables are desired tenderness. Set aside in a bowl.

4 Add a little more oil to the same skillet, then add the tofu. Pan fry tofu for about 2-3 minutes, until crispy. Flip the tofu chunks, and cook on the other side for an additional 2-3 minutes. Repeat until the tofu is crispy.

5 To assemble each bowl, add cooked quinoa as the base, then add cooked vegetables and tofu. Top with red onions, pineapple or mango slices, drizzle with additional barbecue sauce, and garnish with optional toppings such as avocado, coconut flakes or cilantro.

TOFU SCRAMBLE

This simple recipe is a vegetarian favorite. A simple tofu scramble has only four ingredients and can be a tasty plant-based meal for breakfast, lunch, or dinner. Tofu scramble can be served on top of a toast, with a whole grain, in a whole grain wrap, or simply on its own. It's so easy to make, high in protein and only requires 4 ingredients. Customize with added optional ingredients.

Prep Time: 35 minutes
Cook Time: 20 minutes
Serves: 4 people

PHASE　1　2　3

1 block organic, non-GMO tofu (typically 14oz)

½ teaspoon salt

½-1 teaspoon turmeric powder

⅛-¼ teaspoon ground black pepper

ADDITIONAL OPTIONS:

Sauteed onion

Sauteed vegetables: broccoli, spinach, and zucchini work great

Additional spices: garlic, paprika, cumin are all great choices.

1　Drain the tofu and crumble it into a large mixing bowl.

2　Heat a deep skillet and add a splash of olive oil to prevent sticking.

3　If using onions, add to pan and saute until translucent.

4　If using other vegetables, add them to the pan and saute until nearly tender.

5　Add tofu and spices and mix until well combined and cook medium-high heat for 5 minutes. Stir occasionally.

TOFU AND BROCCOLI STIR-FRY

This classic stir fry recipe can be ready to eat in just 15 minutes. Umami is a flavor used to describe this savory, Asian dish. Flavorful and fast, this recipe is one you'll likely turn to when you're short on time--and even when you are not!

PHASE | **1** | **2** | **3**

2 tablespoons extra virgin olive oil, divided

1 container of extra firm tofu, cubed

Sea salt and fresh ground pepper, to taste

1 head broccoli, chopped into small florets, stems discarded

½ cup green onions, thinly sliced

1 teaspoon toasted sesame seeds

SAUCE INGREDIENTS

3 tablespoons tamari sauce

2 tablespoons rice wine vinegar

2 tablespoons raw honey

1 tablespoon cornstarch

1 garlic clove, minced

½ teaspoon ground ginger

1 teaspoon sesame oil

1. Heat 1 tablespoon of olive oil in a large saute pan over medium-high heat.

2. Add tofu and season with sea salt and pepper (a generous pinch of each is usually plenty).

3. Cook for about 5 minutes, stirring occasionally, until tofu is golden brown and slightly crispy.

4. While the chicken or tofu is cooking, make the sauce by whisking together all sauce ingredients.

5. Once tofu has browned, add the remaining tablespoon of olive oil and broccoli, and stir to combine.

6. Continue cooking for another 3 minutes, until the broccoli is bright green.

7. Stir in the tamari mixture, and cook for an additional minute until the sauce has thickened.

8. Remove from heat and garnish with green onions and toasted sesame seeds. Serve immediately.

TEMPEH TACOS WITH AVOCADO CORN SALSA

Featuring chili powder and lime, these tempeh tacos are delicious!

Preparation Time: 30 minutes to marinate
Cook Time: 15 minutes to make tacos
Makes: 8 tacos

PHASE 1

8 ounces tempeh

2-3 tablespoons extra-virgin olive oil

½ teaspoon sea salt

2-3 tablespoons lime juice

1 tablespoon chili powder

1 teaspoon cumin

½ medium onion, diced

¼ cup cilantro, chopped

8 corn tortillas

Shredded romaine lettuce or green cabbage

AVOCADO SALSA:

1 ripe medium avocados, peeled, pitted and diced

½ large ripe tomato

2 tablespoons finely chopped red or white onion

1 clove garlic, minced or pressed

½ cup corn kernels

2 tablespoons fresh cilantro

Juice of 1 large lime

1   Crumble or chop tempeh into small pieces and place in a mixing bowl. Put 1 tablespoon of olive oil, salt, lime juice, chili powder and cumin on the tempeh and mix well.

2   Let stand 10-30 minutes to marinate, (longer time allows more absorption of the flavor).

3   Heat the other 2 tablespoons of oil in a large skillet. Add onion and sauté until soft.

4   Add marinated tempeh and keep mixture moving in the pan until tempeh turns golden brown.

5   If using frozen corn, be sure to thaw kernels first or briefly blanch to hasten thawing. Combine all ingredients for avocado salsa In a medium bowl. Toss gently maintaining chunky consistency.

6   Warm corn tortillas in a skillet with just enough butter or olive oil to move it around.

7   Fill each tortilla with about ¼ cup of tempeh mixture, avocado salsa, lettuce or cabbage.

VEGGIE POT PIE WITH TOFU

Savory vegetables, tofu chunks, biscuit topping...this pot pie is a healthy version of a favorite comfort food.

PHASE 1

1 tablespoon olive oil

2 medium yellow onions, chopped

3 garlic cloves, minced

1 teaspoon salt

½ teaspoon black pepper

1 teaspoon dried marjoram

1 teaspoon dried thyme

2 cups of sliced mushrooms

1 large carrot, peeled and chopped

1 tablespoon of dijon mustard

2 cups sweet potatoes, peeled and chopped into 1-inch chunks

2 cups white potatoes, peeled and chopped into 1-inch chunks

3 cups of vegetable stock

3 tablespoons of cornstarch dissolved in ½ cup cold water

1 cup of frozen peas

1 cup of frozen corn

1 package firm tofu, ½-inch cubed

1 tablespoon soy sauce or tamari

½ teaspoon salt

FOR BISCUIT TOPPING:

2 cups of organic whole wheat pastry flour

½ teaspoon salt

1 tablespoon baking powder

½ teaspoon baking soda

6 tablespoon melted butter

1 cup of buttermilk or plain yogurt

1 Preheat oven to 400°F. Lightly oil 9 x 13 pyrex or casserole dish.

2 Add olive oil to a large pot and cook onions and garlic on a medium heat for 10 minutes. Add salt, pepper, marjoram, thyme, mushrooms and mustard. Cook about 5 more minutes.

3 Add sweet potato, white potato, carrots and stock. Bring to a boil. Reduce heat, cover and simmer until vegetables are fork tender (about 15 minutes).

4 Add dissolved cornstarch to thicken. Add peas, corn, tofu, soy sauce, and salt, stirring frequently.

5 Pour the vegetables/tofu mixture into the oil casserole dish.

FOR BISCUIT TOPPING:

1 In a mixing bowl, combine flour, salt, baking powder, and baking soda.

2 In a separate bowl, mix melted butter and buttermilk or yogurt.

3 Combine wet and dry ingredients with a minimum of strokes.

4 Drop spoonfuls of the biscuit batter over the vegetable mixture.

5 Bake 25-30 minutes or until biscuits are fully cooked.

CRISPY TOFU WITH PEANUT SAUCE

Simple crispy tofu and flavorful peanut sauce make this dish a favorite in our home.

PHASE **1** **2** **3**

1 package of extra firm tofu

1 tablespoon coconut oil

Salt

PEANUT SAUCE:

¼ cup peanut butter

2 teaspoons 100% maple syrup

2 tablespoons soy sauce or tamari

1 tablespoon brown rice vinegar

1 teaspoon grated ginger or
½ teaspoon ginger powder

⅓ -½ cup water

Red chili flakes to taste (optional)
Omit for phase 3

SAUCE:

1 Combine all ingredients in a small pot.

2 Whisk until smooth.

3 Add water to desired consistency.

4 Drizzle over crispy tofu, rice or vegetables.

5 For leftover sauce, simply add water to thin to desired consistency.

TOFU:

1 Drain tofu and wrap in a clean dish towel or paper towels.

2 Place on a tray with a heavy pot on top to press all liquid out of the tofu.

3 On a baking tray, toss tofu with coconut oil and salt.

4 Bake on 400°F until tofu is browned and crispy (about 20 minutes). Shake midway through cooking to brown all sides.

SESAME CRUSTED TOFU WITH GARLIC SPINACH

My sister makes this dish for Thanksgiving every year. It's so good that even the non-vegetarians eat it up!

PHASE   1   2   3

1 package (16-ounce) of extra firm tofu, drained well

¼ cup teriyaki sauce

¼ cup of sesame seeds (mix of white and black is lovely)

1 teaspoon cornstarch or arrowroot powder

2 tablespoons dark sesame oil

2 tablespoons soy sauce or tamari

2 teaspoons of olive or coconut oil

3 cloves of garlic, minced

10 ounces of baby spinach

Salt and pepper to taste

1. Slice tofu lengthwise into 4 rectangular pieces, then slice the rectangles in half to make 8 pieces.

2. Marinate the tofu in teriyaki for 20 minutes to infuse with flavor.

3. Mix arrowroot or cornstarch with sesame seeds in a shallow bowl or plate.

4. Press marinated tofu into the sesame seed mixture to evenly coat all sides.

5. Heat sesame oil in a large skillet on medium heat, add tofu squares in a single layer to cook for 5 minutes on each side. Add soy sauce and cook for one more minute until liquid is absorbed. Transfer tofu to separate plate.

6. In the same pan (no need to clean), add olive oil and garlic and saute for 30 seconds until golden. Add spinach and cook until wilted. Add a teaspoon of water if needed. Season with salt and pepper.

7. Serve tofu on a bed of wilted spinach and brown rice (optional).

EGGS AND DAIRY

Dairy:

Technically, "dairy" refers to the milk from any mammal, but the vast majority of dairy in the American diet is from cow's milk. Dairy products can be a part of a healthy diet for some people, but it is also a common food trigger for many people with lactose intolerance, allergy, or other dairy sensitivity. If you tolerate dairy and plan to include it in your meals, you should only use organic dairy products and move toward fermented varieties like plain yogurt or kefir and small amounts of aged cheeses. Experiment with goat or sheep milk cheeses, which are often better tolerated than cows milk varieties.

For any recipe below that calls for milk, you can substitute an unsweetened plant-based alternative "milk" like almond, rice, hemp, coconut, pea, etc.

Eggs:

Every year, the mainstream media adds to the confusion about eggs. In the 21 Day Revival program, eggs are included because they are a source of high-quality protein, essential fatty acids, vitamins, and minerals. When people transition to a more plant-based diet, adding eggs to your diet 1-2 times a week is reasonable. Choose healthier eggs from free-range, cage-free, and smaller farms instead of those from a large factory farm. This will help ensure higher levels of beneficial nutrients, fewer toxins, and more humane conditions for the chickens.

EGG AND VEGETABLE STRATA

This savory egg dish is easy to make in advance for a weekend brunch or to heat up slices for a delicious breakfast or lunch all week. It adapts well with other vegetable or cheese additions. We like adding artichoke hearts, broccoli, and parmesan.

PHASE 1

1 tablespoon olive oil

1 ½ cup yellow onion, chopped

¼ teaspoon thyme

3 cloves of garlic, chopped

1 pack (8-ounce) mushrooms, thinly sliced

1 bunch of asparagus, trimmed and cut into 1-inch pieces

1 teaspoon salt

12 eggs

1 ½ cups of milk (cow, rice, almond, soy, etc)

2 tablespoons dijon mustard

3 tablespoons parsley, chopped

¼ teaspoon black pepper

4 cups of sourdough bread, cubed

½ cup of crumbled goat cheese or shredded cheddar cheese

1. Heat oil in a large skillet.

2. Add onions and thyme and cook until softened, about 5 minutes.

3. Add garlic, mushrooms, asparagus, ½ teaspoon salt, and cook for 5 minutes, stirring as needed. Remove from heat and set aside.

4. Whisk together eggs, milk, mustard, parsley, pepper and ½ teaspoon of salt in a large bowl. Set aside.

5. Lightly grease 9 x 13 baking dish. Spread half of the bread cubes over the bottom of the dish.

6. Top bread with half of the vegetable mixture and sprinkle with ½ of the cheese.

7. Add remaining bread cubes, then layer with the rest of the vegetable mixture.

8. Pour egg mixture over the casserole.

9. Cover and chill overnight.

10. Preheat oven to 375°F. Bring casserole to room temperature and sprinkle cheese. over the top. Bake about 45 minutes until firm in the center and golden brown on top.

SWEET POTATO WAFFLES

Step up your Sunday morning game and swap frozen waffles for this beta carotene rich treat!

PHASE 1

½ cup cooked sweet potato, butternut squash, pumpkin (canned is fine too)

3 eggs

1 ½ cups milk or milk substitute (cow, soy, rice, coconut, almond, etc)

2 tablespoons butter or coconut oil, melted

1 cup organic all purpose whole wheat flour

½ teaspoon salt

2 teaspoons double acting baking powder

1-2 tablespoons honey

⅛ teaspoon cinnamon

1 Mix sweet potato, eggs, milk and melted butter together in blender or bowl.

2 Mix in flour, salt, baking powder, honey, and cinnamon. Blend together with a minimum of strokes or blender pulses.

3 Cook in waffle iron until golden brown.

4 Top with fruit and plain greek yogurt (optional).

GRAB AND GO VEGGIE EGG MUFFINS

Skip the fast food bacon, egg and cheese! These egg and veggie muffins are a nutritional powerhouse on the go!

(Omit bell peppers and cheese for phase 3)

Prep Time: 15 minutes
Cook Time: 20 minutes
Serves: 6

PHASE 1 2 3

1 dozen eggs

½ teaspoon salt

Fresh ground pepper

Coconut or olive oil to grease muffin tins

CHOOSE 1 CUP OF ANY COMBINATION OF VEGETABLES:

Baby spinach or kale chopped

Tomatoes diced

Onions finely chopped

Red bell peppers finely chopped

Mushrooms finely chopped

Goat cheese crumbles or shredded cheddar cheese (optional)

1. Preheat oven to 350°F. Grease muffin tins with olive oil or coconut oil and set aside.

2. Whisk the eggs in a bowl with the salt and pepper.

3. Saute 1 cup of any combination of vegetables and divide among each muffin tin cup. Sprinkle with cheese (if desired).

4. Pour the egg mixture on top, leaving ¼-inch from the top.

5. Bake for 20 minutes, or until a toothpick comes out clean for each muffin.

6. Remove from oven. Use a knife to go around the edges and pop out the egg cups. Enjoy!

Keep them in an airtight container or place each individual egg muffin cup in a resealable bag for an easy grab-and-go high protein, healthy breakfast each morning. Microwave for 20 seconds for a hot meal.

PUFF PANCAKE WITH FRUIT

This puff pancake is a favorite at our house that we often make for brunch or breakfast for dinner! The batter can be made in advance for quick assembly when time is tight.

PHASE 1

6 eggs

1 1/2 cups milk
(or milk alternative like soy, rlce, coconut, almond, etc)

1 cup organic whole wheat flour

3 tablespoons honey

1 teaspoon Vanilla extract

½ teaspoon salt

¼ teaspoon Cinnamon

⅛ stick Butter or Earth Balance

Fresh or frozen fruit: apples, raspberries, blueberries, peaches, etc

Cinnamon and ½ - ¾ cups of pecans for topping (optional)

1. Preheat oven to 425°F.

2. Melt butter in 8 x 8 Pyrex or baking dish.

3. Recipe doubles easily. If you double it, use a 9 x 13 pyrex.

4. In large bowl or blender mix: eggs, milk, flour, honey, vanilla, salt, cinnamon (ok to be a little lumpy).

5. Put fruit in pyrex on top of melted butter.

6. Pour egg mixture on top of fruit.

7. Optional: Sprinkle with cinnamon and pecans.

8. Bake at 425°F for about 45 minutes, or until nice and puffy. If browning too quickly, cover with foil for last 20 minutes.

9. Serving suggestion: pair with a dollop of plain greek yogurt and a small amount of 100% maple syrup.

HUEVOS RANCHEROS

My Southern Californian husband loves this dish for any meal!

PHASE 1

Corn or flour tortillas

Beans (any type, whole or refried)

Wilted spinach, about 2 cups of raw

Cheese, grated

Cumin or chili powder- optional

Salsa

2 eggs

Hot sauce, sliced avocado- optional

1 On a baking sheet, place 2 tortillas and layer with beans, cheese and salsa.

2 Bake at 350°F until tortilla is crispy and cheese is melted (about 10-15 minutes).

3 While tortilla base is baking, wilt spinach in a pan with a little water, salt and garlic powder. Top tortillas with wilted spinach and fry 2 eggs in the pan. Sprinkle with cumin or chili powder if desired.

4 Top tortilla with fried eggs and add hot sauce and sliced avocado.

YOGURT PARFAIT

Parfaits can be an easy, high-protein breakfast. Get creative with your favorite toppings! For a parfait on the go, try adding frozen fruit. When it melts, the liquid from the melted fruit sweetens the yogurt nicely. And don't forget to pack the granola separately in a small container to add in when you are ready to eat if you like some crunch!

PHASE `1` `2` `3`

**Plain yogurt
(greek, whole milk, or low fat)**

Fresh or frozen fruit

**Granola (look for less than
12-grams of sugar per serving)
use gluten free for phase 3**

Nuts/seeds/flax/chia/coconut

**Drizzle of 100% maple syrup
or honey**

1   Add ½ - 1 cup of yogurt to a
    bowl or container.

2   Choose your favorite toppings.

3   Layer as desired.

VEGETABLE FRITTATA

Frittatas are a very forgiving dish. Add leftover roasted vegetables like broccoli, sweet potato or butternut squash or start with fresh veggies, lightly sauteed. (Omit peppers, tomatoes and cheese for phase 3.)

PHASE 1 2 3

2-3 tablespoons olive oil

1 yellow onion, chopped

2 cloves garlic, minced

8 eggs

1-2 cups of chopped vegetables (any type such as broccoli, zucchini, mushrooms, red peppers, cherry tomatoes, spinach) or leftover roasted/ steamed vegetables (sweet potato, broccoli, etc)

½ teaspoon salt

¼ teaspoon black pepper

Fresh herbs:
parsley, dill, basil-optional

½ cup cheese--grated cheddar, feta, or goat cheese--(optional)

1. Break eggs into a large bowl and beat with a whisk. Add salt, pepper and any fresh herbs.

2. Heat a 10-inch skillet with an oven proof handle over a medium heat on the stove top. Add olive oil and onions, stirring until onions are soft and starting to brown. Add garlic and cook for 1 minute.

3. Add vegetables and saute for 2 minutes.

4. Add vegetables to the egg mixture and stir in cheese (if using).

5. Clean and dry the skillet and add return to a medium heat. Add 1 tablespoon of olive oil once hot and swirl to coat the skillet.

6. Pour in the egg/vegetable/cheese mixture and cook undisturbed over medium heat for 3-4 minutes until eggs are set on the bottom.

7. Transfer skillet to pre-heated broiler and broil for about 3-4 minutes, until frittata is firm in the center.

8. Serve warm or at room temperature.

SPECIAL SECTION FOR LIQUID ONLY FAST DAYS

The 21 Day Revival includes a short, liquid-only fast section as part of the program. Liquid nutrition for 48 hours is a safe and effective way to jumpstart your anti-inflammatory biochemistry without compromising your nutrition. Your immune system uses vitamins, minerals, and phytonutrients for fuel, so optimizing the absorption of these compounds is an excellent way to enhance the anti-inflammatory process.

The recipes listed below are for teas, broths, soups, and smoothies that give you maximum nutrition with minimal digestive effort. Feel free to experiment and add or subtract ingredients to your own preferences. Your blender is your friend and your artistic canvas!

NUT-BERRY PROTEIN SHAKE

PHASE **1** **2** **3**

1 cup frozen fruit (blueberries, strawberries, raspberries)

1 tablespoon almond butter

1 tablespoon of chia seeds

1 tablespoon hemp seeds

2-3 raw walnuts

1 tablespoon pumpkin or sunflower seeds

¼ avocado

1 cup unsweetened milk substitute (hemp, pea, rice, coconut, almond)

1 teaspoon of honey

1 Combine all ingredients in a blender and blend on high until desired consistency.

2 To thicken, add more frozen fruit. To thin, add more milk substitute. During non-liquid days of the plan, you can also make a smoothie bowl by using this shake as a base, and top with fresh fruit, granola or coconut flakes.

MISO BROTH

Miso soup can be hearty with added vegetables and tofu, but during the liquid phase of this plan, simply mix miso paste into hot water for a comforting broth to sip.

PHASE 1 2 3

4 cups water

1/3 cup white miso

Dash of gluten free soy sauce or tamari

1 Heat water in a small saucepan until almost boiling.

2 Remove from heat and stir in miso.

3 Add a dash of soy sauce or tamari to taste.

CARROT GINGER SOUP

PHASE **1** **2** **3**

1 organic onion, sliced	1 teaspoon cumin
1 inch ginger, peeled and sliced	1 quart organic veggie stock
1 tablespoon coconut oil	Sea salt and pepper to taste
2 pounds organic carrots, peeled and chopped	

1 Sauté the onion and ginger in the oil in a medium saucepan until soft.

2 Add the carrot slices and cook for 5 minutes.

3 Add remaining ingredients and simmer for 45 minutes.

4 Puree the soup in a blender then season to taste and serve warm.

BLENDER GREEN JUICE

Not everyone has a juicer, so this easy recipe uses a blender.

PHASE 1 2 3

1 1/2 cups water

2 cups kale

2 green apples, cored

1/2 cup parsley leaves

1 medium cucumber, quartered

2 celery stalks, roughly chopped

1 inch piece of ginger, peeled

2 tablespoons lemon juice

1 Add all ingredients to a blender and mix on high until liquified.

2 Enjoy. Or if you do not like the texture of the pulp, for a less "chunky" juice you can strain through a mesh sieve.

HIBISCUS TEA

PHASE 1 2 3

6 cups water

1 cup dried hibiscus flowers

Sweeten to taste with stevia or a small amount of honey

Wedge of lime- optional

1 Bring water to a boil in a medium saucepan. Add hibiscus flowers. Remove from heat, and let stand for 1 hour. Strain through a sieve to remove flowers. Sweeten to taste.

2 Refrigerate for at least 1 hour before serving. Add a squeeze of lime-optional.

LEMON GINGER DETOX TEA

PHASE 1 2 3

1 teaspoon fresh grated ginger

1 tablespoon of fresh lemon juice

1 cup hot water

½-1 teaspoon raw honey or maple syrup to taste

Small pinch of cayenne-optional

1 Boil water in a kettle.

2 Add fresh squeezed lemon juice, grated ginger to a mug and add boiling water.

3 Allow the lemon and ginger to steep for 5 minutes, and then sweeten to taste. If you like a bit of spice, add a tiny pinch of cayenne.

CARROT APPLE ICE BLEND

This refreshing juice is cool and sweet.

PHASE **1** 2 3

1 cup carrot juice

1 cup unsweetened apple juice

1 tablespoon fresh lemon juice

1 ½ cups of ice

1   Add ingredients into a blender and blend on high until liquified.

POMEGRANATE-CHERRY SMOOTHIE

Flavonoid rich pomegranate and cherries make this smoothie recipe a tart, sweet, heart-healthy treat!

PHASE 1 2 3

1 cup frozen pitted cherries

3/4 cup pomegranate juice

1/2 cup plain organic yogurt

1 tablespoon honey

1 teaspoon lemon juice

pinch each of cinnamon and salt

2 cups ice

1   Add all ingredients into a blender and blend on high until desired consistency.

TROPICAL SMOOTHIE BOWL

Sometimes smoothies are more fun to eat in a bowl! Smoothie bowls are simply thicker smoothie mixtures that you can eat with a spoon. Adding nuts or seeds and coconut on top add nice crunchy texture. (omit for liquid only fast days)

PHASE 1 2 3

2 cups non-dairy milk (coconut, hemp, almond, pea, soy, rice)

1 frozen banana

2 cups frozen pineapple

1 cup frozen mango

1 teaspoon pure vanilla extract

Pure maple syrup or honey to taste

1 tablespoon roasted pumpkin seeds, sunflower seeds, or raw nuts

1 teaspoon shredded coconut

1. Add non-dairy milk, banana, pineapple, mango, vanilla to a blender and combine until smooth.

2. Add a small amount of maple syrup or honey to taste if needed.

3. Pour into a bowl and top with nuts, seeds and coconut during phase 1 and 2

PEANUT BUTTER SMOOTHIE

A classic combination of nut butters and banana. Vegan, creamy, and delicious.

This recipe can be made like a milkshake or a smoothie consistency with the addition of ice.

PHASE 1 2 3

1/2 cup non-dairy milk (hemp, coconut, almond, rice, soy, pea)

1 tablespoon all natural peanut or almond butter

1 tablespoon cocoa powder

1/4 medium avocado

Stevia to taste

1/4 cup ice or frozen banana- optional

1 In a high-speed blender or food processor, add all your ingredients, except the ice or frozen banana, and blend well.

2 If the smoothie is too thick, add enough milk to reach your desired consistency. If too thin, add some extra ice or frozen banana.